26 Ways to Grow Your On-Line Business

By

The Learning & Earning Center

&

26ways.com

All Rights Reserved 2014 The Learning &
Earning Center

We have done our best to provide accurate and informative information for everyone reading this book. But since everyone is different and everyone's situation is different as well, all or parts of this book might not be applicable to everyone. It is up to the reader to ascertain the suitability of the information according to their own application and situation. The writers, producers, and sellers of this book assume no responsibility for the use or application of any or all parts of this publication.

Contents

One: Know Your Customers	5
2: Overcoming the Online "Hurdles"	21
3. Reinvest in Your Business	39
4. Capture their Excitement!	41
5. Bring in the Right Kind of Customers or Visitors	45
6. Specialize	51
7. Become an Authority	57
8. Advertising	65
9. Offer Complimentary Products	73
10. Diversify Your Monetization	79
11. Design for Multiple Visits	88
12. Reach a Broader Segment of the Market	92
13. Utilize Social Marketing Ads and Resources	100
14. Go Video!	106
15. Form Alliances with Other Marketers	117
16. Open Multiple Locations!"	123
17. Deliver Amazing Value	127
18. Build a List through FREE Products!	132
19. Using E-Mail as a Sales Tool	137
20. Create a Blog	145
21. Include Reviews or Testimonials on Your Site	155

22. Outsource It!	160
23. Brick & Mortar Stores	165
24. Franchising	167
25. Avoid Over Extension	169
26. Do Something You Love!	175
In Conclusion	179

One: Know Your Customers

This is one of the most important thing yet many marketers and business owners fail to address this when planning and growing their business.

The customer should always be our primary focus because we need them in order to be successful and remain successful. I don't care how good your product is or what your price point might be, if no one purchases your products you will not remain in business. It is that simple.

It is also important to understand why people buy your products. Do they buy them because they "want" them like people buy televisions and IPADS and other products or do they buy them because they "need" them like they purchase food and gasoline?

Knowing why they purchase the products will give you a huge insight into how to best market and present them.

All businesses need new customers in order to grow or even stay the same size. People pass away or lose the need for certain products as they get older. For example, if you sell kid's toys, those kid's you are selling to today will become teenagers in a few years and you will lose them as customers. If you sell products for the aged or elderly, a certain part of your customer base might pass away each year simply because your customers are older than the customers for other businesses. So the result is that almost every business that wants to grow or expand has to not only replace the customers that leave but also attract new customers.

What all of this means is that the business owner needs to know what their customers are looking for and then design his or her business to provide as much of that as possible to the customer. This is what marketing is all about. Letting the people know everything you and your products have to offer them. That is the only way people will be attracted enough to visit your website or click on your product links.

It is no longer good enough to offer great products. There are just too many alternatives for customers these days.

30 years ago people were limited to whatever the stores in their local or neighboring stores sold. Today they are just a few mouse clicks away from hundreds or thousands of vendors looking to sell them their products. While this is great for the customer, it makes it harder and harder for those looking to make sales.

We need to create even more value in order to set ourselves above all the other businesses out there that are targeting the same customers. We need to show people that we have the best deal, the best products and the best overall value for them.

But we can never prove that if we don't understand what our customers are looking for. We can never give people more of what they need or want until we understand what they need or want. This is so basic and so simple that it is amazing how many people don't take the time to do this.

Though the buying reasons will differ from product to product and even customer to customer, there are a few basic needs and reasons that seem to hold true for the vast majority of our customers.

These should form the basis for designing your best customer experience.

Though this is far from an all-encompassing list, it should be enough to get you started:

Customers Want to Feel Secure

Before most people purchase online, they need to reach a certain "comfort level" with the business they are purchasing from. The "big boys" on the block with all that name recognition already have gained that trust through their reputation. But chances are that you are not at their level yet so you have that obstacle to overcome.

The best way to overcome that obstacle is to reassure the customer that you are there for them whenever they need it. That means having a phone number or at least an e-mail address on your website. An address is a great thing as well if you have a brick and mortar store. This way they can see how they can reach you should they have a question or problem after they purchase.

Name brand products are also a huge advantage when it comes to gathering trust. While people might not trust your business name they will recognize and trust a name brand product.

That is because they know that they can always go to the manufacturer if they have problems. So if you can, especially in the beginning, stock and sell name-brand products that inspire trust and confidence.

Another good way to inspire confidence is to provide some kind of money back guarantee to your customers. This reassures people that they will have some time to evaluate the product to make sure it really is what it was marketed to be on your site. After all, when you buy online, you cannot actually touch and hold the product. You have to rely on pictures and descriptions which might not be totally accurate!

Customers Want their Problems Resolved

This is the primary reason why anyone purchases anything in this world. Every purchase has an issue or problem behind it. People buy products to solve problems.

So it stands to reason that the more problems your products will resolve the more customers you will attract.

For example, people buy a television because they want to watch programs and without a television that can be very difficult. They buy a car because they need to drive from one place to another for various reasons. They buy toilet paper because life with toilet paper is much better than life without it! Behind every purchase is a problem or situation that this product or service addresses and resolves.

If you want to grow your business and make more sales, stop selling features and benefits and start selling solutions. Start marketing and presenting your products as solutions to certain common problems. People don't care about a washing machine that has 31 speeds. But if that machine and all those speeds washes clothes faster and gets them cleaner, that's what they are most concerned with!

Studies also show that people are far more interested in solving problems than they are about the price they have to pay. So if you can show them how your product can solve all their problems, closing the sale will be a piece of cake!

Many sales people and business owners get so caught up in the features and benefits that they forget why the product is even in existence! EVERY product that has ever been built or manufactured has addressed a problem or a need. No one ever designed anything that had no practical use or accomplished nothing through its existence! So if the main reason something was designed in the first place was to address a need, should those who sell it take that approach as well?

Which of these approaches do you think would have the greatest chance of resulting in a sale?

"Mrs. Smith, this television has a 190 degree dispersion angle and a 200 watt sound amplifier built in. It also has 1080P and a wide range of input types. Would you like one?"

Or,

"Mrs. Smith, this television has a 190 degree dispersion angle which means that even people sitting on the side of the screen will see a fully detailed picture. That can be a problem with other televisions. Also, the 200 watt sound amplifier will bring depth and feeling to movies and videos.

It also has a wide array of inputs which means you will be able to connect your DVD, video game consoles and even your computer to this television. That can be convenient and so much easier than having to purchase adapters and other equipment later. The 1080P resolution will give you a picture that is so detailed and lifelike you will be amazed!"

The second approach gave the features but explained how those features solved problems or made things better. It described a problem (sitting at the side and seeing a dull picture, listening to weak sound or seeing fuzzy or blurry pictures) and how this television addresses all those issues and more.

This helps paint a picture in the mind of the customer of how this product would make their lives better, easier and more rewarding or enjoyable. That can prove to be a powerful incentive to go ahead and purchase the product. The customer's mindset plays an awfully big part in their decision whether or not to purchase.

When you sell features and benefits, you are selling things most customers might not relate to.

In that approach you are counting on the customer's ability to take those features and benefits and connect them with their problems and needs. A lot can go wrong with that approach. But when YOU concentrate on resolving problems instead of just rattling off features, YOU are making that connection for the customer.

You are making absolutely certain that the customer understands how this product is going to make their lives better, solve all or most of their problems and why they need to purchase this product from you right this minute.

Customers Want Value for their Money

This is something we will say several times in this report but customers are normal people just like you and I. Therefore, they want pretty much the same things as you and I would like and one of those things is that we expect to get value whenever we spend our hard earned money.

No one is eager to purchase when they feel something is overpriced or for some reason not a particularly good deal.

We have in our minds a certain level of value that must be met before we will commit to purchase the product or service. If that level of value is exceeded, we are more likely to purchase. If that level is not reached, we are far more likely to walk away and look elsewhere.

It is also important to state that value is not the same as price. Granted price is an important factor in deciding whether or not to purchase but it is not the only factor when it comes to value.

Value includes the product itself and how well it is made, the things that it can do and certain other factors that might include the type of warranty, available accessories, ease of use, size and several other factors.

Customers will also consider other value added services such as free delivery, free installation, free training and other things they can get from you when they purchase.

These value added extra's might have a low value to you but a high perceived value to the customer. It is not so much the actual cost of these extra's that matter. What really matters is the value the customer places on them that counts. Free delivery makes everything easier for the customer.

Free installation means a lot because the customer does not have to install the product or find someone who can. This particular service can have a very high perceived value for the elderly.

So if you want to grow your business and increase your sales, give some serious thought about what you currently can offer your customers. Look for ways to add value to each and every product or service that you sell. Look to add things your competition doesn't offer so you are set above the rest. If you can create more value, you will create more sales.

It really is that simple.

Customers Want Convenience

Almost every customer wants an easy way to purchase what they need. They want to walk in, find their product, pay for it and walk out in as little time as possible and with the least amount of inconvenience. No one intentionally loves to purchase at places where everything is a pain in the neck and takes forever.

With that in your mind, look for ways to make purchasing easier. Make sure your products are easy to find and located in places where people expect them to be. It is well known that the average attention span of most people is measured in seconds so you only have a short time to get the customer to where he or she needs to be.

Have a well-designed website and webpages that are clear and easy to understand. Make it easy to read about the product and see the features and benefits. In the product description tie those features and benefits to common problems that they solve or address.

If a product pertains to more than one problem or area, make sure that product is listed in all those locations. Doing this will also make your product line look bigger at the same time. The goal should be to make products easy to find. The search should be intuitive which means that it should be easy for people to get to the products they need without wasting time and getting frustrated.

Customers also want it to be easy to pay for whatever they want to purchase. If they have to go through 42 steps in order to buy something, they might just give up.

That's why the larger sites have one button purchasing, save customer information and do other things to make things easier and faster.

So take a look at your business from a customer point of view and see how you can make things easier and streamline your policies and procedures. Making it easier for people to find your product and purchase them will allow you to close more sales, increase your income and grow your business faster.

Customers want it NOW!

We are all pretty impatient when it comes to purchasing things and waiting for our products to arrive. We all pretty much want things immediately. No one wants to wait a day or a week for their products to arrive. We want things yesterday and it is not going to change. We are who we are and we better get used to it!

This means having the products your customers want and having them in stock for immediate shipping. For some digital products that might mean instant delivery through e-mail or automatic download.

For physical products is might mean offering one day shipping to those who are willing to pay the extra cost.

It is important to remember that when people shop online it is not like they have to drive an hour or more to see if someone else has something in stock. All customers have to do today is make a few clicks on their mouse. If you are out of stock but someone else has the same item in stock, you have just lost a sale.

Make sure your stock is adequate so that when you reach a certain stocking level and you reorder that the new shipment arrives before your stock runs out. Granted there will be times when you have an unexpected demand for certain products and you will run out but do your best to make those situations a rarity.

Look for any way you can to deliver your products and services as quickly and easily as you possibly can. This is something most customer really don't think about but it is still very important to them. Only when you don't have something do they think about it and by that time, it might be too late to lose a sale!

Customers Want after Sale Support

Customers want to feel secure that their problems will be resolved and their questions answered after the sale has been completed. This means have a customer service procedure and method of contacting your business for after sales support.

People who buy products will have questions and there will be defective products. Even the best and most high quality products will have defects and require service or replacement. With a brick and mortar store the answer is easy. You simply walk back into the store and exchange the product. For an online store or business the process is more complicated.

If you want to improve your business then you need to make after sale support a priority and have processes and procedures in place to address concerns, answer questions, and supply information regarding replacement or servicing of the products that you sell.

At a minimum you should have a phone number or e-mail address that is monitored so that these issues and questions can be answered.

This will go a long way in assuring the customer that they will not be forgotten once the sale is made and payment has been given.

While we will discuss this shortly, keep in mind that your customer cannot see your business and can only go by what your website looks like. So they look for ways to get a better "feel" for your business and having contact information goes a long way towards making the customer feel that your business is a legitimate one.

2: Overcoming the Online "Hurdles"

We all know the advantages of opening an online business. We don't have to purchase real estate or pay rent for a brick and mortar building. In some cases we don't have to stock inventory or pay a lot of fees and taxes that are part of the brick and mortar model of business. You can start an online business in an hour or so by just creating a basic webpage and putting it up on the internet. So' starting and operating an online business is much easier and cheaper than starting a brick and mortar business.

But because of this, all kinds of people, many of which have no idea how to run a business, are starting web-based businesses and offering shoddy merchandise, poor customer service, and even engaging in illegal or at least suspicious behavior.

This results in angry customers and a generally poor opinion of all but the largest and most established online businesses.

So let's just agree that there are some hurdles the online business owner is going to have to overcome before he or she can take their small business and grow it into one of the "big boys" over the next few years. Though the actual obstacles or hurdles will vary depending on the market you are in or the products you will, here are some of the most common or generic hurdles you will have to remove in order for your business to grow:

Is Your Business Legitimate?

Since it is so easy to start an online business, many people enter the online marketplace with less than honorable intentions. Just from looking at a website, one cannot possibly know whether this business is a legitimate business or just someone working out of his bedroom closet!

With a brick and mortar business you get a sense of permanence.

You think that they are legitimate and will still be there when and if you have problems. A website is just a website and once it is gone you have no way of ever getting in contact with them again.

Some so-called "businesses" are just people selling other people's products and doing and saying things that are not designed to help the customer but just sell the product. There are so many of these "businesses" today that it is getting harder and harder to just find information on the web today let alone accurate information. It seems that everyone is trying everything in order to capture a sale.

Because of this, there is a high degree of skepticism among most customers today when it comes to purchasing from online businesses. You need to look at your business and figure out ways to instill that confidence in you and your business. Especially in the beginning, do not concentrate so much on selling as you do on creating trust and confidence with those who visit your site. Once you have accomplished that you can start concentrating on selling.

Can Your Business Be Trusted?

As an online business, you are pretty much anonymous. You can put any picture or any information you want on your website and no one is going to know any difference. Customers know this and are naturally hesitant to purchase products from people they do not feel they can trust.

It used to be that testimonials were used to establish trust but even those are sometimes falsified today. So the online business has to deal with this kind of issue every day.

The best way to establish trust is through a spotless reputation but this can take years to establish. So the best thing to do is provide a clear and well defined warranty and return policy and then adhere to it. Provide excellent customer support and service and resolve all problems quickly.

In the beginning, before you are well established, concentrate on how you accept payments. Checks are clearly more work and delay the fulfillment of orders.

Accepting credit cards is a great way to pay because every card has a protection feature that guards against loss and misrepresentation. Sometimes this alone will give people the confidence they need to purchase from you.

As we have already said, make sure there are at least two ways for customers to contact your company. Placing both a phone and an e-mail address on your website can go a long way in reassuring a customer. If you cannot place a phone number on your site make sure you check the e-mail account several times a day so you can respond to e-mails quickly.

It is also important to understand that trust is something that is built up slowly but something that can disappear immediately if you do something wrong or treat a customer poorly. Make every effort to handle disputes or complaints quickly. Answer all questions and inquiries as quickly as possible as well. The longer you take to respond the more time the customer will have to believe you are not someone who can be trusted.

Lack of "Touch & Feel"

One of the main advantages of shopping in person is the ability to touch and feel the products. You can actually see and feel the quality of the product as well as its appearance and size. When you shop online, you need to rely on pictures and descriptions that are sometimes very inaccurate.

Descriptions can be crafted to make things better than they really are and pictures can be taken in such a way as to make the product appear larger or smaller or better than it really is. I am sure that everyone has received something through the mail that was totally different than what we thought or expected.

Customers usually like to use as many of their senses as possible when it comes to choosing what they purchase. It must be visually appealing and it must feel and look well-made and durable. You cannot tell those things from a picture on a website.

In order to compensate for this many customers will shop locally to see and touch the product and then go home to check out the prices online.

In order for an online business to capture these sales the price and overall customer experience must compensate for the lack of touch and feel as well as for the delays involved in shipping the product to the customer.

Related to this are the customers who will see and like a product advertised on your online website but then go out and try to find it in a store so they can actually see the product in person. The dangers of this are that if the customer finds the products locally they might buy them locally and not where they first saw them which was on your website!

To help compensate for the lack of touch and feel we need to provide more detailed information and realistic descriptions and accurate pictures. You see the big sites like Amazon furnish all that information and much more including dimensions, product reviews (supposedly from actual buyers) and detailed descriptions for potential buyers to read.

This can be an even more difficult problem for websites that feature their own products not available in stores or from other retailers.

Confronted only with pictures and a description many customers will not purchase a product they have never seen when manufactured by a company no one has heard of.

Lack of Intimacy & Interaction

Online businesses also do not have the personal interaction that we have when we walk into the store. This is both a plus and a negative for most online businesses.

Lack of personal interaction is considered a plus because most people do not like to be bombarded by sales people or pressured into purchasing a product. Most people want to be helped but no pressured. With an online website, people can stay as long as they want without be bothered or pressured to purchase. (As long as the site does not bombard them with pop-up boxes and offers.)

But this can also be a negative because it is this personal interaction by the sales people that help us determine exactly what the real needs are and to choose the perfect products for the customer to purchase.

When you purchase online, only you get to choose and you might pick the wrong product.

The personal interaction is where online websites can come up really short in the eyes of the customer. Most customers are not that knowledgeable on every product and some of what they do know might be inaccurate or totally wrong. Though talking with the salesman this information can be revealed and the customer counselled as to what product is right for them.

Some websites have instituted real time chat rooms where customers can get support or questions answered by live agents through their computers. This not only allows the customer to talk to people and get answers to their questions, it also helps the business become more accessible and foster a higher level of trust with their customers.

Convenience Issues

This is another area where there are plusses and minuses associated with online businesses.

Nothing can beat the convenience of just sitting down at your keyboard, doing a search or two and then viewing a few websites to see what is the best product for your needs. That is certainly a lot better than driving all over town trying to get information that might not exist!

But buying online involves shipping and shipped takes time. So there is almost always a delay in getting physical products into the hands of the buyer. Digital products can be delivered instantly through automatic downloads which is an advantage for the web-based business.

As we have already stated, customers want what they purchased right now. They do not want to wait days or weeks for their products. In order to reduce the effects of this problem, an online business needs to process and ship orders quickly and promote that service to their prospective customers. Though this will not completely resolve the "instant gratification" issues with some customers, it will help.

It is suggested that you find ways of delivering merchandise to the customer as quickly as possible.

Utilize drop shipping, overnight delivery, or in the case of digital products, instant downloads. Anything you can do to get products into the hands of the buyers faster will help your business grow.

Apart from actually delivering the products, online businesses have another problem that brick and mortar stores do not have. That problem is informing the customer that the sale actually did go through and their merchandise ordered.

Think about it for a minute. When you pay in the store you get a receipt for your purchase. When you click a button online, you really have nothing that lets you know that your order has in fact been placed. For all you know you could wait for days or weeks only to find out that your order was never fully processed!

To address this issue, all online businesses should capture e-mail addresses and instantly send a receipt or order confirmation to every customer who places an order. This will not only reassure the customer that the order has been placed but will also provide them with a record should they have a need to follow-up with anyone in the future.

Though these are but a few of the problems facing on-line businesses, there will be more depending on the products you sell and the customers you serve. Generally speaking, the more expensive the item or product is the more hesitant the customer is going to be ordering it on-line if they do not trust the on-line vendor.

The level of proof of legitimacy for on-line business is much higher than for other types of business and this is as it should be. Every time you read or hear of a story where someone has lost money due to an on-line scam, or every time someone is cheated on-line, every on-line business suffers and pays the price.

If you truly want to grow your on-line business you must put safeguards in place to protect your customers. You must also practice good business practices and always behave to the letter of the law. Your reputation as a reputable on-line business is at stake every time you have to deal with a customer. Exercise the utmost in caution and try to do the right thing by everyone.

When problems occur, and they will occur no matter how thorough we are and how hard we might try, we need to act quickly and resolve the situation to the customer's satisfaction.

Only by addressing things quickly and resolving them properly can we maintain our good reputation.

This is very important because once you lose a good reputation, it can take a long time to get it back. Sometimes businesses never recover and eventually fail.

Think & Plan for the Long Term

Many people start their business and plan their business for right now. New businesses are more concerned with the here and now than they are about what might happen 10 years from now. But that places them in a trap that could come back to bite them big time if they are not careful. So if you are looking to grow your business or take it to the next level, you must act and plan for not only what happens today but also for what might happen 10 years from now.

Sometimes you will find yourself in situations where you might find yourself making one decision if you only think about today and a totally different decision if you take the future into consideration. So your viewpoint and focus does matter and you need to focus on the right things in order to make the right decisions.

Many times the actions we take today can have a profound impact on our business tomorrow or next year. We might anger a customer today and have that customer tell 100 of his friends about it and that could cost us big time in the years to come! Growing businesses need to look at every decision for both short and long-term ramifications.

Let me give you an example:

Ben owns a deli in a large business complex. He does a pretty good business especially at lunch. He is also trying to start a catering business. One of his first catering jobs doesn't go exactly as planned because it was, after all, his first catering job.

His customer comes back to him and tells him of the problem and asks for some of their money back.

Ben balks at that request because the problem was a minor one and giving back what was requested would mean he would lose money on that job. Thinking short-term, Ben decides he doesn't want to lose money on the job so he just apologizes and rejects the refund request.

Naturally the customer is unhappy and goes back to their office and re-tells the story to other people. Word spreads from office to office and eventually almost everyone hears about the problem and how it was handled. Another local deli gets all of the future orders because of the negative reaction to the story.

The bottom line is that Ben saved a few dollars today but placed the future at risk. So let's take another look at the same story and how it could have been handled differently.

Ben gets the refund request and instead he offers to cater the next event for free to make up for the problems that were just experienced. This winds up to be a better deal for the customer and they accept. Ben pays special attention to this new job and everything turns out wonderfully!

The customer is happy and word soon spreads on how great the event was handled by Ben and how they stood behind their products and services. The end result is that Ben now gets most, if not all, of the catering work for the office complex primarily due to how he handled a bad situation.

In this example Ben gave the customer even more than what they asked for and the result might have been a short-term loss but a long-term windfall from all the additional work that came from the positive comments about how this situation is handled. So long-term Ben didn't lose money at all! In fact he gained a ton of business out of a bad situation!

We always need to take a look at how any decision might affect us short-term and also for years down the road. We need to make sure the decisions we make will serve us well now and also later. We also need to be able to understand when it might make sense to bite the bullet now in order to get a benefit in the future.

Nowhere is this truer than when trying to determine the real value of a customer. The real value of a customer is much more than the value of their last purchase.

Their real value must also include the value of his or her expected future purchases and the value of the purchases made by others who came to buy from you because of their recommendation or word of mouth advertising.

For example, if we use Ben's deli again and Betty buys a $5 sandwich every day for lunch, her customer value is not just $5! If she buys 5 sandwiches a week for 50 weeks that comes out to $1,250 a year PLUS all the people that Betty might recommend the deli to!

If you think about customer value in that way, it should definitely change your attitude towards your customer!

In the example of Betty, if you valued her business at just $5, you might tell her to go elsewhere if she didn't like her sandwich and wanted a refund. But if you realize that she represents $1,250 worth of business a year to your deli, you probably would go ahead and make her a brand new sandwich or give her the money back. Why? Because potentially losing $5 in business is a lot different than losing $1,250 worth of business!

People who look into the future and prepare for it are the ones who see the most growth and the most success. People who look to the future and make decisions taking it into consideration usually also find it easier to keep up with things as well. We cannot live just in the present. We must take advantage of the opportunities of today while preparing our business for what is going to happen tomorrow.

Which brings us to the next item on our list………..

3. Reinvest in Your Business

Growth of any business requires money and time. Every good business owner understands that in order for a business to flourish you have to reinvest part of the profits back into that business. And this should be happening consistently, not just once in a while or when expenses back up.

Under capitalization is one of the reasons many businesses fail. You always need to have the resources available to you in order to move a business forward. When it comes to expansion this is even more important because expansion takes money NOW but usually will not result in increased profits until LATER!

If expansion is in your plans for the future discuss with your accountant NOW how to best prepare for that. Though financing is sometimes the answer, financing costs money and might not be the best route for a business to take. Carrying excessive debt is dangerous and if a little bit of planning now will help you a lot later, it is best to do it now.

There is another type of reinvestment that helps growth or expansion and that is to reinvest in your employees or workforce. Expansion takes talent and you should have the people in place to handle the increased workload and responsibilities. This might require additional hiring or retraining in order to have the necessary manpower to move forward with the projected growth. Growth that happens before the staff is capable of dealing with it can actually set a business back considerably and it can take a long time to recover from those kinds of setbacks.

I cannot stress just how important proper planning and investment in time, money and resources is to any growing business.

4. Capture their Excitement!

Business growth requires customers who are ready and willing to buy your products and services. Depending on the products and services you sell, and the market you are selling within, this can be either very easy or extremely difficult. Because of this, you have to do your best to capture the attention of your customers and make them want to go to your website.

There are several ways that you can go about bringing people to your website. But once you get those people to come to your website you need to capture their attention and create some excitement or enthusiasm for your site and the products or services that you sell.

You do not have a lot of time in which to accomplish this either. Most people will "graze" over your home page to see if anything interests them. If, during those few seconds, you do not capture their interest, they are likely to stop looking and go on to some other site. It makes no difference if you have the perfect product or service for them on another page because they will never get that far. If you cannot capture someone's interest from your home page you have lost the battle for their attention!

In order to capture someone's attention, you have to have a kind of "hook" on your home page. You have to show them that your product can fill their specific needs, solve their problems or make their lives better or easier. If you can accomplish this then you have a chance. If you fail at convincing them they just move on.

This usually means having some kind of content on the "above the fold" part of your home page. That is the part of the home page that first comes on your screen before anyone scrolls down. In other words, everyone sees this content when the page pops on the screen. If this content makes people curious or excited, they will scroll down to read more. If not, they move on.

This is important because not everyone will scroll down. If your page looks boring or is not interesting, people will have no desire to read even more boring content. So don't save your best for the bottom of the page. Whet their appetite for more by giving them something great to make them curious.

Give them hints of a great product or offer or the promise of something for free if they take a look inside. Whatever you do and however you do it, your focus right now is getting people to go into your website to see what you have to offer.

The more excitement you can generate the more your customer will think about how your products can help them in their life. The more they think about your product the more likely they will be to buy. So in other words, excited customers are far more likely to buy from you.

Create a headline that draws people into your page. Use a sub headline to sharpen the hooks and draw them in even further. Make them aware of what problems or needs that your product will solve for them. The more problems you can solve and the more needs your product address the more likely your customers will buy from you.

Use realistic and true testimonials so your customers can see how pleased and impressed other people were about your products. People love to see validation from others for making the same purchase. It reassures them that they are making the right decision and are purchasing the right products. But make sure the testimonials are truthful and legitimate. Do NOT make them up or falsify words!

Whatever you do, your focus at this point should be to make your customer want to read more of your pages. You should want to make them feel like they HAVE to read it or that they will miss something important. When you achieve this people will continue to read more and more until they either purchase.

5. Bring in the Right Kind of Customers or Visitors

There is a saying that says that all businesses need customers to survive and grow. Well, I disagree with that statement. I think the statement should be "Every business needs BUYERS in order to survive and grow!"

You see, all buyers buy but not all customers turn into buyers!

You can have 500,000 customers visit your website but not make a single sale. So you have a ton of customers but no buyers.

Buyers help pay the bills and generate profits. Customers do none of those things until they turn into buyers!

This is not to say that customers are not important because they certainly are. Customers who do not buy today might buy tomorrow or next week so you cannot and should not ignore them. But we should try to bring as many of the RIGHT customers to our website so we stand a better chance of converting them to customers!

For example, if I own a company that sells skateboards and I get 500,000 senior citizens to visit my website that means I have 500,000 customers that I have almost zero chance of turning into buyers! After all, there are not many 95 year old skateboarders around these days!

But if I brought 10,000 teenagers to my site, I would stand a much greater chance of turning some of them into buyers of my skateboards! That is because the type of person I brought to my website are the type of people who buy my products!

In web marketing we refer to this as "targeted" vs "non-targeted" traffic.

Targeted traffic means you are bringing people who fit a certain type to your website. They might fit a certain demographic such as age or sex or have certain interests. In other words, these people fit the overall model for your most common buyer.

Non-targeted on the other hand means that the people being directed to your site are not evaluated or screened in any way. They might be young or old, male or female, rich or poor or married or single. This kind of traffic is kind of a "crap shoot" but it is cheaper than targeted traffic. But cheaper is not always better and in the case of traffic, it is NOT better!

If you can get FREE traffic from a blog or some other source, then it really doesn't matter what kind of traffic it brings to the site because you are not paying for it. Or are you? Any time you generate traffic from any source, it is costing you time and it is costing you bandwidth.

Bandwidth is the amount of data your web hosting company uses to host your site every month. The more page views or the larger the webpages, the more bandwidth or data you will require.

Some hosting accounts have limited data while others will allow you to have all the data you require.

Usually data is not a problem but you should check to see if you do have limits. If you do have limits check to make sure you are not approaching those limits each month.

Exceeding the data limits may result in shut down of your site for the rest of the month or penalty charges.

It also costs you time to set up even free traffic. You have to go to the site, sign up for the traffic and enter all kinds of site data and sometimes personal data. If you are going to spend that time on generating traffic shouldn't you concentrate your efforts on bringing the right kind of traffic?

Go to relevant sites or sites that you know attract the same kinds of customers that you are looking for. For example, if you sell products for the elderly, you might want to place an ad on the AARP website or something similar. If you sell hobby products, then go to sites where people go for hobby information. It's not rocket science but it does take time and effort to do it right.

There are services that will send you traffic for a fee and those might be good options for you if the service is legitimate. Try smaller amounts of traffic at first with a few of these services and see which ones give you the best results. Do one at a time so you know which traffic you are getting.

But also be careful because some of the services will send brand new customers premium traffic for their first order. These are their best or freshest leads and their best buyers. They send this to first time buyers because they know people test services with small orders first. So they send you traffic that buys your products so you send them a large order and you get no buyers. I'm not saying all services do this but some do so be careful. Your best bet is to place a slightly larger order next time and a slightly larger order after that. This might help you get better traffic.

Your best traffic, though is going to come from referrals or word of mouth advertising. These are customers of yours who recommend your website to others. They might do this on a forum posting, a blog post, or on social media. Wherever the mention of your site appears, it will be seen by others.

We will be talking about this more in upcoming chapters but for now, keep one thing in mind. The best traffic you can bring to your site are people who have a known need for the products you sell and are willing to purchase online.

Any other type of customer you bring to your site is far less likely to buy your products. Do not waste your time and money attracting people who will not buy from you. This ties up resources, possibly slow your website down and cost you money in the long run.

6. Specialize

Some people think that they will make more sales if they stock a wider range of products. This makes sense to many people because the larger the audience you appeal to and the more products you have for them, the more likely they will be to find something they like or need and buy from you.

But online businesses are different from brick and mortar stores. When you have a physical presence in an area you get walk-in traffic. These people might be curious about your store or it catches their eye as they drive by and they stop in to take a look.

But online businesses get much of their traffic from search engines and for search engines, they like to see high value for specific needs or products when they rank those sites. If you are selling everything from toilet paper to high end jewelry, your site will not have a high ranking for any one item.

For example, if you have a 20 page website dedicated to nothing but model airplanes, that site will rank much higher for the term "model airplanes" than the same 20 page website selling model planes on one page and unrelated products on the other pages. The dedicated site might make the top 1 or 2 pages on the search engines whereas your multi-product site would be buried on page 4,567. In other words, no one will ever see your site in the search engines.

A more important reason for specializing is that people come to your website for three things. They come for knowledge, expertise and products. In other words, they come to your site to get questions answered, to learn something new about something and to find products that address some of their needs.

They are more likely to find this kind of information and value on a site dedicated to just the one topic.

There is also a perception issue in that when a visitor to your site sees just one type of product, they will feel that they are far more likely to get an expert or at least informed opinion on the products and information provided on the site. If they see a wide range of products featured on a site they will feel that no one can possible be an expert, or at least informed, on everything and they will look elsewhere. We will talk more about this in the next chapter.

In order for you to grow your business you need to give your customers a reason to come back to your site more than once. This means updating your content so there is always something new and interesting on your site to make people want to bookmark it and return later.

No business can grow, let alone stay in business, if it has to constantly replace old customers with brand new customers. This is extremely costly and time consuming and takes away valuable resources from the rest of your business.

Ideally your specialty should be something you know a lot about and are interested in.

The content that brings people to your site is the content that they cannot find anywhere else. This content includes personal experiences, personal observations, your insight and any tips or tricks you have learned by actually using the products on the site or participating in the specialty or activity.

This kind of information can only come from people who are involved in the area of expertise. If you are in this are just for the money, you will either have to hire someone with this expertise or find some way of getting new content that is fresh, unique and interesting.

One word of caution, however. There are people out there that tell you how easy it is to get content. How you can go out and take other people's articles, change them around or "spin" them, and then post it on your site. While you can do this, be aware that this content is not "special" to your visitors. Chances are if you found it and are using it other sites have done so as well. This will hurt your site in two ways.

First, the content will not be special and your visitors might not think highly enough about it to bookmark your site so they can come back later.

It will also damage your sites credibility to the point where people might question the commitment or knowledge of the business and therefore find it less trustworthy. There are a ton of those kinds of sites out there and you do not want to be bundled in with them!

Second, the search engines monitor content and compare it with content already out there on other people's sites. If your site is just reposting or recirculating old or existing content, that will hurt you in the search engines. Your content should be original, it should be accurate and it should be timely.

This does not mean that you cannot take someone else's article, read it, and then write your own summary in your own words with some of your own thoughts in it. You can copy a subject but you should not copy an entire article.

Think about it from a customer's point of view. If you were to land on a site and see copies of the same articles that you have seen on other sites, would you feel this was a valuable site?

Or would you feel that this site had little to offer and was just a site focused on selling you products while providing little or no additional value?

Think about one last thing when it comes to specializing and providing information on your website. Many people visit sites when they are not in the buying mode or even before they start looking for a product. They visit the site because they have a need or curiosity for knowledge. If your site is deemed valuable for providing that knowledge and some special insight, they will come back. Then, when they are in the mood to purchase they will come back to your site because they have developed a certain amount of trust in you and your site.

This is a critical factor is expending one's business. By developing relationships NOW through the providing of information and knowledge, you are setting the stage to be chosen for purchases LATER. This is a fundamental process in establishing your business in the eyes of customers. Most people never buy on the first chance. They come back several times before they decide to purchase. Whether you get the sale or not depends on how you meet the customer's needs during those first few visits and the perception you help create.

7. Become an Authority

When you specialize in one type of product or in one particular area of expertise, you also have the opportunity to position yourself as an authority or expert in that particular field. Just like we talked about in the last chapter, your customers need or want knowledge and they want to find places where they can get that knowledge.

So much of the purchase process depends on trust and security and when you position yourself as an expert or authority in an area you almost always create trust and security in the minds of the customer.

When this happens they will pay closer attention to your suggestions and recommendations and will also feel better and more secure on the products you offer for sale on your website. But becoming known as an authority on anything requires more than just a great website with informative content.

In order to become an authority or well-known expert you have to put yourself out in front of the customers. That means coming to the customer and not waiting for the customer to come to you. You want name recognition and that only comes from repeated exposure to the same customers. Very few people buy on the first contact unless the purchase is low cost and risk free.

For example, I might run into a store to purchase a roll of toilet paper or a quart of milk but I will go to several dealerships before purchasing my next car. The more expensive or important the purchase, the more legwork and investigation will go into it.

So how do you get your name out in front of the customer and get them to come to you instead of the other way around? There are several ways to do this and those ways are growing all the time.

But here are a few to help get you started and get your thinking:

Social Media

Social media has evolved into one of the most important and lucrative ways of promoting your business. You can have a social media following for your own business and develop a list of followers. These followers would be directly interested in your particular area of expertise and the products that you sell. This is highly targeted traffic.

You can publish posts or tweets that instantly go out to others and even more important, those posts and tweets can be rapidly shared between friends on these networks. You could post something now and have it seen by millions in a few days or hours if the information is interesting!

Blog Posts

If you can find blogs that are in the same industry or area of your expertise, consider posting your comments about recent posts or other articles and topics.

Do NOT use these posts as sales pitches but instead concentrate on providing information to the reader. Most posts allow a website link in the signature so if people like what you have written they might click over to you site to see what you have to offer there.

Initially it might take a while to search out the best blogs or see which ones are the most popular but after you have done so, the more your name gets out there the more people who will see it. Even if they don't realize it, your name will sound familiar when they see it elsewhere and eventually they will equate all of this exposure as proof that you are an expert or well-known member of this particular community.

Don't spam these blogs with constant posts or the owner of the blog might ban you. The same goes for selling in these posts. Keep it all about the information and leave the sales pitch at home.

Forum Posts

Much like blog posting, forum posting can help you as well.

Comments and contributions to forums can go a long ways in helping establish you as an expert or authority in your area. Keep your replies relevant and topical and again, leave the sales pitches at home.

Your goal should be just in getting your name out there along with your link and hoping that people like what you wrote enough to visit your website. Even if they don't visit directly, when they do happen to come across your website, it will have name recognition because of your posting in forums and blogs.

Videos

Videos have come a long way in getting exposure for you and your website. Creating videos and placing them on YouTube and other video sharing sites is a great way of introducing yourself to other people with common interests.

Create a short video on a specific topic or area of interest and post it with your website link. If people like your videos, they might visit your site!

Another great thing is that people can place YOUR videos on THEIR websites if they feel that your message has value. So people on other websites are actually promoting you whenever they promote their website!

Articles

Writing articles for various publications is a great way of establishing yourself as an authority or expert in your field. You can write the article, get it published and then refer to that article in blog posts, advertising and other venues. Being a published author will help you immensely in securing your reputation as an expert!

Depending on your particular expertise writing articles for publication can sometimes be a pretty lucrative way of earning money as well. Although this usually comes after you have established yourself, even novice writers can score a payday for writing an article!

If allowed by the publisher, always include a link to your website either at the end of the article or in your author's biography.

This helps tie you to your website and vice versa.

Volunteering

Volunteering your time and knowledge to charities or other events is a powerful way of getting your face and name out in front of a lot of people. There is no better way of becoming well known than getting out there and helping others and becoming associated with such a worthy cause.

But just like in blog and forum posting, do not go into your sales pitch. Just concentrate on helping others, helping the cause, and becoming known in the community. Eventually others will get to know you and that's when the magic happens!

With all of these methods, it is important that you use them for the write reasons. You should want to spread your knowledge and you should want to provide valuable and useful information to others. If you are doing all of this just to make a few more sales and earn a few more dollars, this will not work.

This is also not a method or process that works overnight although sometimes it can. Usually the exposure happens over a period of time and gradually starts to provide value and show results. If you think all you need to do is make a couple of posts and customers will start hammering down your doors, you are likely to be disappointed. But if you are serious in wanting to establish yourself and your business as experts, all of these efforts are well worth the time and resources.

8. Advertising

Last, but certainly not least, comes advertising. Advertising for an on-line business is different than advertising for a brick and mortar store. When we advertise for our online business, we are trying to get our customers interested in our website. Once we get them to our website, then we try to get their name and e-mail address.

We mentioned before that few people purchase on the first visit to a store. Well, on-line customers sometimes take that rule to the utmost limits. Since it is easier to visit an on-line store than a brick and mortar sort, people tend to require more visits to on-line stores before they purchase. Somewhere in the range of 8-10 visits before people purchase is not unheard of!

So our advertising focus has to be a little bit different when it comes to our on-line business. We have to advertise to both bring short-term buyers to our site, interested people to our site, and long-term buyers to our site. If we are to grow our business, we MUST target ALL three types of customers.

Short-term buyers are people looking to or already ready to buy. For these customers we need to bring our product offerings to them so they are aware of what we have to sell. For these buyers prices might be an important consideration as well as product lines and features. Also, advantages and reasons for buying from us rather than elsewhere are important. Stressing items such as free delivery or shipping or value added extras designed to convince people to buy now are important. Those are the factors that customers ready to buy value most.

For long term buyers, we need to stress information, selection and reasons for purchasing through our business rather than somewhere else. For long-term buyers, information on the products is critical because they are still in the "investigating" stage and are still trying to decide what to buy.

So providing information pertaining to features and application can be critical. Also, article on how to choose the right product or just information on the type of product itself can help create confidence in both the product and the website. Our focus is not on closing the sale now, but to get the customer to come back when they are ready to purchase.

Interested people are those people who are interested in what we have to offer but have no desire to purchase at this point. Maybe they are interested to learn more, are just curious, or are at an entry level and are looking to become more educated so they can make the right purchase when they are ready.

Interested people can be anyone from the "newbie" to the veteran who is looking to learn more or just get more involved. They might even be people who used to do something or be involved in something a while ago and are looking to get re-engaged. Either way, they are looking for information and advice and we need to target them as well and provide what they are looking for.

Regardless of what type of customer we bring to the site, short-term, long-term or interest customer, we need to get all of them to do one important thing for our business. We need to know who they are so we can contact them later. That means grabbing some personal information from everyone who visits your site.

Getting people to give you their personal information, even just an e-mail address, can be difficult. Especially in this day and age where scammers and spammers are harassing everyone, every day. So if we want someone to provide us with their e-mail address, we usually will have to give them something of value in return.

That "something" might be a newsletter that provides weekly or monthly information or perhaps discount coupons or other ways of saving money on a future purchase. It might be a free E-Book or some other product that has a somewhat high value to the consumer. Whatever that value is, it should be sufficient for the customer to willingly provide you with their e-mail address.

This information is important because if you get 100,000 people to visit your website and don't make a single sale, then those 100,000 visits have done your business no good whatsoever. Granted some might return but most will not unless they see significant value in what your site had to offer.

But if you had their e-mail addresses you could contact them later one with information, discounts, product releases and host of other things. This is where the value comes into play!

Your advertising needs to develop customers who will buy now, customers who will buy later, and identify people that you can target to get their business in the future. If your advertising only addresses one or two out of the three then your business is missing out on a ton of value from those who want to purchase your products now or in the future.

Even though this is not a book on advertising, as far as business growth is concerned, advertising will play an important role. So with this in mind, it is important that your advertising convey all the advantages you offer to your customers that other businesses do not.

This is usually referred to as your "Unique Selling Position".

You Unique Selling Position is what sets you and your business apart from everyone else. It represents all the reasons why your customers need to purchase from you and no one else. Customers do not always notice all of these things. You almost have to hit them over the head with them to get them to notice!

If you rely on the customer to figure all of this out on their own and draw the right conclusions, well, then you will be missing out on a lot of sales! You cannot leave anything to chance when it comes to drawing customers into your business and closing those sales.

The bottom line is that if you offer something that no one else does, that is an advantage for you. But if the customer is not aware that you offer this, or if they are not aware that no one else offers it to their customers, that advantage flies out the window!

If the customer is not aware of an advantage in doing business with you, it is no longer an advantage.

The customer might go to another store and pay for delivery because they weren't aware that you deliver for free! So they wind up spending more money and you wind up losing a sale. Instead of a win-win resolution, you created a lose-lose!

Make sure your advertising adequately portrays your Unique Sales Position. Make sure if let's every type of customer understand why they should buy from you or visit your website. Don't rely or expect them to realize this all on their draw. Instead, lead them through every advantage and every reason you have that they should but from you!

It is so easy to go from website to website these days you need to give people a reason to visit your and stay on your site once then land on it. If you have information on your site that should interest people, make sure they realize that. If you have a great line of products, make sure they know it. If something is on sale, make sure they are aware of that as well.

In order to reach the most prospective customers, you have to have an advertisement that offers something for everyone. Spend the time and resources you need to create this kind of advertisement.

It might take more time and money to create the perfect advertisement but it will bring you much better results and earn you much more money.

And whatever you do, put something in place to capture the e-mail address of everyone who visits your site!

9. Offer Complimentary Products

Many business and many salesmen do a great job identifying customer's needs, selecting the right products and closing the sale. While all of that is great and will help a business become successful, there is one more thing that could be done that could really help the business increase profits and grow even faster.

That is making sure to offer complimentary products to your customers.

Next to closing the highest percentage of sales, the size of each sale is just as important to the overall growth and prosperity of any business.

While there is a limit to the number of available customers for any business, there is no limit on how large each sale can be. So the key to business growth and prosperity is selling more to the same number of customers.

We can accomplish this easily through the selling of complimentary products or more commonly referred to as "add-on" sales. Add-on sales are items the salesmen or website recommends to customers to improve, enhance or make possible the full enjoyment of the purchase of the original product.

This has been a staple of doing business for years but it is still amazing how many business fail to grasp this simple concept. Some businesses are hesitant to try and sell more items to the customer because they do not want to badger or annoy the customer and possibly lose the sale all together. But that is the wrong attitude because add-on sales actually can help raise customer satisfaction instead of lowering it!

It all depends on the attitude and approach of the webpage and business.

The suggestion of add-on products should always be focused on what is best for the customer. If the add-on product will make the customer happier, make things easier or more convenient, or make them more satisfied with their original purchase, that item should be suggested. If selling the item would just increase the commission while doing nothing for the customer, it is best left alone.

Sometimes add-on sales really help us out and make their purchase more enjoyable. For example, if someone purchases a DVD player the website might say something like "Would you like an HDMI cable with that? They do not come with one and you will need it to connect it to your television." If the customer needed one they could buy it right then instead of going home, be disappointed that they couldn't connect their new DVD player and have to go somewhere to purchase the cable. If they already had the cable, they could just say no and they would not be annoyed or upset. The same thing does for other non-supplied accessories such as batteries, cables, ink, paper or whatever else might be required for that product.

Customers do get annoyed when non-related products are suggested or many products are pushed onto the customer. For example, if someone wants to buy a pack of batteries and you try to sell them a television, then a DVD player, then headphones, then a washing machine, followed by a cell phone plan, a computer and a camera, then the customer would probably just abandon the order and shop somewhere else.

But if the suggested items will benefit the customer, there is no reason why they should not be suggested. Start off with the most obvious products like batteries, ink and closely related items not provided with the product and then proceed from there. Always give the customer a chance to proceed directly to the checkout. The desired end result should always be to make the customer happier with their original purchase.

Add-on sales are also usually more profitably for the business as well. Profit margins on most products today are razor thin while profit margins on accessories and other related items are much larger. So it is not unusual for add-on sales to generate more profit than the primary sale!

Plus, the expenses of the primary sale, the product itself, the cost of providing the salesmen and support personnel as well as advertising expenses have already been "paid"! The profits from those add-on sales are just icing on the cake!

If growing your business is one of your primary objectives, then it makes sense to monitor not only grow sales but the add-on sales as well. Because sometimes it is these small add-on sales where considerable profits are generated. We should always be aware of the amount of add-on sales our webpages generate.

Suggested add-ons can be programmed into the product listings or listed on the same page as the main product. You could include a suggested accessories" listing next to a "What's in the box?" listing so that customers would be aware of what they are getting and what they need to use the product. All of this should be done in a nice and easy going manner which does not make the customer feel angry or frustrated. Keep in mind that when people purchase on-line they are far more ready to just exit a page in mid-order when they get annoyed. It is must less awkward to that on-line than it is to do that in-person!

Another form of add-on sale is to use follow-up e-mails to people who purchase certain products to inform them of other related products or special sales that they might find useful. After all, they have already shown their interest by purchasing one product from you. Why not go for more?

This is where many business concentrate a lot of their earning power. Fast food places have been doing this for decades! Anytime someone says "Do you want fries with that?" is trying to generate an add-on sale.

Shouldn't your business do the same?

10. Diversify Your Monetization

One of the primary differences on-line businesses have from brick and mortar businesses is that an on-line business can earn money even without selling products! We can do that through a practice more commonly known as "monetization".

Monetization refers to all the different ways a website can be used to generate income or earn money for the owner of the website. There are many ways for this to happen. A good business website will not rely on just sales to generate income but also integrate other methods as well. The desired result is the generating of income both when customers purchase products and also when they do not.

Here are just a few ways a website can generate income without the sale of the actual products and services that it markets:

Ads

Some websites host ads on their sites for similar or complimentary products. Then, either when ads get clicked on, or when products are purchased, the owner of the website earns a fee or commission. Depending on the type of ad program you are participating in, you will either be paid for displaying a certain number of ads, paid every time someone clicks on the ad, or paid each time someone purchases a product or takes a specific action from that ad.

Depending on your overall traffic volume, the income earned from these types of ads and programs could be substantial. But there are certain factors that the website owner must understand when using this type of revenue generator. These concerns are mentioned a little later in this chapter.

Pay per Click

Pay per click ads are ads that you display on your website for your customers to click on. When someone clicks on these ads from your site you are paid a commission. This can range from a few pennies to a few dollars depending on the ad and subject matter of the ad.

It should be noted that some website owners take underhanded steps to get their visitors to click on their ads. Most pay per click ad programs have strict rules and monitor content and clicks very closely to detect fraudulent behavior. Accounts can be terminated without warning and any accrued commissions forfeited if fraud is encountered. Usually when this happens account holders are banned for life so be very careful.

Pay per Action

Pay per action, or cost per action, are ads that pay you a commission or fee whenever someone purchases a product, signs up for something or completes a certain defined action. When a customer does what is required, the referring website owner earns a fee.

These fees, though much harder to earn than pay per click, are usually much larger than pay-per-click and if you get the right offer and you have the right customers, can result is considerable income. The same concerns and warning for pay per click also apply to pay per action.

Pay per View

No, this isn't like ordering movies on-line! This is getting paid for displaying a certain number of ads, usually in batches of 1,000. For every 1,000 ads displayed, you earn a small fee regardless if your visitors purchase anything or take any action.

This usually has the lowest income but it is income that is generated by nothing other than displaying the ads. Used in the proper context, this can give you some income but not all that much so that you can sustain a business from it. This kind of income must usually be combined with other forms of revenue.

Referral Products

Referral income is when you display an ad for another person's product and you get a percentage of the price whenever someone purchases it from your link. If you find the right product, and expose it to the right people, referral links can generate a LOT of income. So much income, in fact, that there are businesses that are completely sustained by referral income!

The positives with referral income is that you don't have to actually sell or develop products and you don't have to worry about fulfilling orders or any of that kind of stuff. You just refer to another vendor and take your commissions.

There are many services such as Clickbank and JVZoo that allow you to open an account and promote thousands of other people's products for commissions. As we said, if you find the right product and sell it to the right people, you can make a good income through referral sales. If you have an established mailing list, you can send out referral offers to your list to generate income whenever you want.

The downside of monetization is that you have other products and services competing with your products and services on your website.

If you have good and relevant ads hosted on your site, those ads are bound to take away some of your visitors from your webpages and this can hurt the sales of your own products. With commissions usually less than what you would make selling your own products, this can hurt instead of help your bottom line.

I always recommend that you set up any ads or links on your pages for other people's products so that they open up in a brand new browser window. You can usually specify this in the link properties box in your web editor program. When you have the links open in a new window YOUR window remains on the browser so when the new link is closed, your site is still there. Sometimes when people click on links that take over the existing window, they forget how to get back to your site. Having new links open in new windows eliminates that problem.

But the website owner must always keep in mind that ANY other ads on their site can possibly siphon away buyers of YOUR products and direct them to sellers of THEIR products. You must decide if you are willing to lose the attention of a possibly buyer for a few pennies earned from a pay per click or pay per view ad.

For example, if you send 1,000 viewers to an ad that pays you 10 cents per click or view you would earn $100.00 in revenue. But if it costs you 25 lost sales on which you would have earned $25.00 per sale, you would have lost $625 in sales! That's not a great deal if you ask me.

The best way to diversify the income earned by your site is to offer diversified products all relating to the same field or industry. In other words, try and have something for everyone who might visit your site. Always make the focus of your site on YOUR products and services. Keep any ads or other forms of monetization to non-competing products or services that you do not offer. Try and lead the customers who seem to be looking for those types of products to that link instead of showing it to all your customers.

If there is a referral product you are promoting, consider tying that to an article or webpage designed to discuss and provide information on that particular area and then feed the customer to that affiliate link.

This way your customers are driven towards your products when you have something to offer and to an affiliate product when they are looking for something you don't offer that is related to your specific area or industry.

Monetization should always be geared to promote your products first and then selectively guide the other customers to where they have the best chance of finding something relevant to them. Not only will this please and satisfy the customer, who has been searching for this knowledge, it helps keep your core customers away from other products and convincing them to purchase YOUR products instead.

This is not to say that competing products should never be promoted. They should be promoted but to customers who purchased your product already and then the other product promoted AFTER the original sale!

For example, someone purchases a book on how to set up a WordPress business site from you. After the sale you can send them to an affiliate link for WordPress templates to make this task easier.

This way you sell your own product and use the affiliate link or ad as an add-on related product. If you just placed the ad on your webpage, the customer might have purchased the templates first and not had the urgent need to purchase your product. So you would earn pennies instead of a lot more.

Monetization is a way to generate more income that everyone who is looking to grow their business or increase their income should consider. But it should be part of a marketing plan that is well thought out and directed to produce the best overall results.

Good monetization is carefully laid out in a flow that promotes your products first and foremost and then creates additional selling opportunities. If done correctly, it will not reduce your core sales while increasing revenue generated from secondary sources. When done wrong, it can reduce overall revenue by replacing low commissions in place of higher profit sales. Design your monetization on paper as a type of flow chart that lets you know where your customers should be directed at each stage of the sales process. Then program your webpages and place your ads and revenue sources appropriately.

11. Design for Multiple Visits

You have a dynamite website that really captures the interest of most of your viewers. You have great content, an attractive way of presenting that content, and a flow that engages the customer and keeps their attention. Website designers would say that you have the perfect trifecta. That is great content, great interest and keeps their attention. Many would say that this is all you need to capture sales from your customers.

And they would mostly be wrong.

While every site needs to have great content, a great flow or design and capture and keep the attention of the viewer, a truly great website needs to have one more important design element.

It needs to make people come back again and again in the future.

As we have stated before, the vast majority of people looking to purchase rarely purchase the first time they visit a site. This is especially true for the first time they purchase from any particular site. They need to feel comfortable. They need to be reassured in your business. They need to develop trust. These customers might require up to 10 visits before they actually purchase from you.

That is why you need to keep your content changing and growing so there is a reason for someone to re-visit your site even though they might not be looking to purchase anything at that time. In other words, they should be coming back because they WANT to not because the need to. There should be something on your site that keeps them informed or keeps them wanting to come back to see what's new!

That is why people keep coming back to Social Media and blogs and forums. They keep coming back to see who has just posted the latest information or who has responded to a particular question.

They come back because there is always new information. They come back because there is always something new to learn or something new going on somewhere with someone.

Websites need to have constantly changing content. Customers look for it, search engines demand it to keep high rankings and it gives the website the appearance of being a resource instead of a sales oriented website. Few people come back to see what you are trying to sell them today but a LOT of people will come back to see what you are teaching today. That is a huge difference that every business owner needs to be aware of.

Websites, depending on their industry and products, should update their content at least once a month but more often is better if you are able to. Add an article weekly or provide advice or a featured product link to help people see something new when they come back. The change should be evident on your home page because most people will not look further if nothing appears fresh or new since last time.

Your webpage design should be targeted to get people to stop and visit, hold their attention while they are there and to give them something that will draw them back in the future. Good, solid and changing content will do that while at the same time making it easier for your customers to see your site as a valuable resource and see you for the expert you should be trying so hard to become known as.

12. Reach a Broader Segment of the Market

If you want to expand your business, that means expanding your customer base. After all, it makes no sense to expand into other areas if the end result is going to be zero growth. The only time that would make sense is if your existing customer base is rapidly decreasing and you need an influx of new customers to stay afloat.

But when it comes to bringing in new customers, this almost always requires reaching a broader or different segment of the marketplace. This might mean a larger geographical area or trying to appeal to a different demographic.

A perfect example would be a store selling baby products and furniture. There is a limited age group for which those products are appealing to parents and after that, they leave to purchase products relevant to older children and teenagers. But if you want to capture that market and keep those existing customers longer, you might entertain expanding your product offerings to products for that older age group.

The results would likely be that you would now appeal and cater to two different market groups. The group you always had plus the new group with older children. So now instead of having customers for 3-4 years, you might have them for 10 years!

This is assuming that your store continues to specialize in those market segments and does not all of a sudden lose focus and try to appeal to everyone all at once. No matter what you do it is important to always retain the core values and focus that enabled you to be profitable and successful all those years.

But things to do change and market demographics are no different. As neighborhoods change so do the people who live in them.

Depending on the products you sell and the areas you sell to, those demographics might benefit or hurt your business.

When this happens you need to take action as required. If they benefit you then you need to expand to take care of the extra sales and needs of your customers. When they go against you it is time to adjust and bring in new customers to make up for the shortfall. Changes are not necessarily a reflection of what you have done right or wrong, they are just an indication that something has changed and that you need to get out in front of that change and not be consumed by it.

When it comes to on-line businesses. This would mean changing the focus of your marketing to perhaps reach customers who might have never even known your site existed. Maybe these customers were just outside your area of specialty but close enough to have a need for your products if they knew your website was out there.

In order to reach new people, you have to market your business in different directions.

This means advertising on new websites, changing your search terms or search engine optimization to include new search terms geared for new customers or it might mean changing where you post and blog.

In order to reach a broader market or a different market you usually have to update and modify your content as well. If you are attempting to reach a new segment of the market then you will need to have content relevant to those customers in addition to content for your existing customers. You must not sacrifice the customers you now have in order to bring new ones into the business. That would defeat the purpose of trying to get more customers in the first place.

In some cases we can have multiple websites or different starting or home pages for different types of customers. You would send your links out according to the marketing you might have for those customers. When you take this approach customers are sent first to the directly relevant content designed specifically for them. This helps capture their attention quickly without hurting other customers.

When you take this approach, make sure to have the other areas of your site, the ones with the rest of your content, easily accessible with links showcasing that content. Many customers have multiple needs which might make then attractive to multiple areas of your site. Using the example of the baby store, perhaps one set of parents has a 9 year old and a one year old. In that case they would need products for both age groups not just one.

Last, but most certainly not least, sometimes it will be necessary for a business to change their products or focus in order to replace products whose life has come close to the end or whose interest has slowed over the years. When this happens the business really has no choice but to adapt and change with the times.

The best way to deal with demand changes is to be out in front of those changes. That means knowing your products and knowing which products are selling and which products are not. It means knowing if certain products are selling better or worse than last year and spotting trends in the beginning rather than at the end.

Proactive changes generally make it a lot easier for businesses to integrate certain changes. By gradually replacing poorly selling products with new products, the product line can undergo slow and almost invisible changes that customers might never recognize. This allows the focus of the business to gradually change as well and during that transition you might find yourself with two sets of customers. The original customers who like the older products and new customers attracted to the new products.

If you wait until sales forces you to make the change then the massive changes necessary to keep your business solvent could alienate existing customers before new customers become aware of what type of store you are now. This is especially true with on-line stores which depend largely on word of mouth and search engine traffic. If all of a sudden you product line and focus changes, your site could take a nose dive in the search engines and you might lose customers. A well designed and planned gradual change would be much better for your overall search engine ranking.

Reaching new customers is always important and who you reach out to and how you do it are very important. You need to think this out carefully and make the transition gradually and seamlessly with alienating existing customers in the process. Keep in mind that your goal is MORE customers not just different customers.

On-line businesses can change product lines more quickly because there are not physical products to move or large inventories to deal with like in other stores. Most of the changes involve website design and content and those changes can be made with your editing software and once everything is complete, uploaded to your site. There is no really "work in progress" for on-line sites like there are for physical businesses and that is a big plus.

So take your site, determine what changes are necessary for you to reach more people, and come up with a detailed and well thought out plan for reaching those customers. Remember that you need new content, new products and new site design to attract new customers. Without either one of the three your efforts are much more likely to fail.

You cannot just add products to attract new customers. You must add new content to support those products and to provide information to those customers who are looking for it. Content is what brings back people time and time again in the future and we need that to eventually generate sales.

Broadening your market is one great way to grow your business very fast if you go about it the right way. But it requires thought, planning and the correct execution to pull it off properly and get the best results.

13. Utilize Social Marketing Ads and Resources

Make no doubt about it, I dislike Social Media. I see so many people waste hour after hour posting pictures of what they ate for dinner, creating stupid videos and wasting all kinds of time that should have been spent actually talking to and interacting with real people in person. But while I feel that way, I also realize the importance of using Social Media for your business. So I guess you don't have to like something to realize its value and use it.

Social media started out as a way for people to interact together easily on line and also to meet people in their community or through other people they knew.

But it has evolved into a business marketing tool as well. With more and more people gravitating over to social media, every business should have a presence on the major social media websites.

Businesses can use social media to announce news pertaining to their business or industry as well as new product additions, current sales, and even the sharing of information relevant to the industry they are involved in. As you develop a list of "followers" for your business, this can help you spread information quickly and increase the response to sales, discounts and other promotions resources.

But wait, it gets even better!

One of the great things about social media is their ability to take your post or comment and make it "go viral". That means having the information on your comment or page be sent to unlimited numbers of people, some who you might never be able to reach otherwise, through the sharing by your followers! The exposure can reach into the millions and it's all for free! Social Media could very well become a major force in your marketing!

Here is how it works:

You create a business page and do some basic promotion. Place a link on your webpage to Facebook, Twitter and some of the other social media networks. Also send out an e-mail to your customers making them aware of your presence on those sites. They go to the site, click on the link to "follow" you site and then every time you post an entry, they see it on their home page.

The difference between social media and e-mail is that most people check their social media pages several times a day. So they see your latest post or news very quickly and they can't easily delete it like they might an e-mail. (They can ban you or "unfriend" you though so be careful!)

If they like what you have sent them, they can share it or "like" it and that means all their followers will see it as well. So you might only have 10 followers but if each one of those followers has 100 followers, your message goes out to 1,000 people if everyone shares it. 990 of those followers you might not even know but they will read about your site now! And some of those 990 people will share your message to their friends as well. So it keeps spreading further and further and further without any effort on your part!

In order for this to work well for you, there has to be content that your followers think highly enough about to share it with their friends. The content could be an article, video, another web link to valuable information or anything else that your followers feel has value to them and to others.

If you send out crap or endless sales messages, you will quickly be dropped or "unfriended" and few people will see your message. But if you can product quality content that has value, social media can spread your message faster than many other sources.

This will be semi-targeted traffic as well which is good to have. I say semi-targeted because while your followers have shown an interest in what you have to offer, all of their follower might not have the same interest. But if your follower shares it to their followers, it is because they feel it will have value to them. So the results should be pretty good if you use this correctly.

You can also purchase ads on social media sites as well.

While not as good as a comment or post from your website that appears on someone's home page, these ads do get seen and a lot of businesses make a lot of money off of these ads. This is just another advertising resource that should be tried and refined to see if it works for your particular business.

Social media is the perfect "word of mouth" type of advertising venue. The best thing about it is that it makes it so easy to share your message to millions of people. People tend to do things more if they are easy to do and one click is about as easy as it can get! A little work in the beginning can create a powerful network for your business.

Start by placing links to popular social sites on your webpage and make it easy for your visitors and customers to click on them and follow or join your page. Send out e-mails to your current customer list letting them know you are on these sites and give them links to your new pages so they can follow them as well. This will jump start your network and get you going.

Over time people and the social networks themselves will recommend your site to others and your following will grow.

As long as people see value to what you are offering, your network should continue to grow. Once people stop feeling your content has value you network will start to shrink.

Once you have started on social media, set aside time each week to manage your social media sites. Upload current content and keep yourself in front of the eyes of your followers. Do not bombard people with posts and comments. This is a major turn-off. But a few times a week, or even once a day if you have enough valuable content, will help keep your followers interest and engaged.

One word of caution regarding social sites: They are very aware of businesses using their services as nothing but a sales tool and if you do not adhere to their rules they will ban you from their sites! Always read the rules of conduct and their rules for site content and obey them to the letter. This is NO place for black hat or underhanded sales tricks! There is just too much to lose by skirting the rules to get an extra couple of sales.

14. Go Video!

Video scares a lot of business owners because they don't feel that they have the skills or talent to create or even star in their own videos. Because of this they stay away from them and can miss out on some very powerful methods of gaining the interest of their customers and closing some sales.

But the great thing about using video is that it makes it so easy to capture the interest of the customers. When you place a video on your website and set it to start or play automatically, the customer is drawn to that video whether they intended to or not. As long as the video starts off by grabbing the attention of the viewer, they will at least give the message a chance.

Videos are also great for actually showing a product in use or how to set-up or use the product. For on-line businesses this is great because people do not have the luxury of seeing the product and touching it or feeling it let alone seeing it work. But a video can show that what the product looks like, how large or small it might be and how well it works.

It has been said that pictures are worth a thousand words and if that is true then a video must be worth a million words because they can be that powerful. The downside of video is that they are more difficult and time consuming to make but that should not frighten any website owner away because there are different ways to get videos for your site.

Here are a few ways to get a video for your site:

Make them with a Video Camera

Any digital video camera can be used to create a video for your website. Just shoot the video of the subject while adding your own commentary or audio track and upload it to your computer and then to your website.

The video can be as basic or as fancy as you have the capability and desire to make it.

The y should use an interesting or attractive background but the background should not be a distraction that gets in the way of the message. Use a tripod is possible so there is little to no shaking which can make it more difficult to watch the video. You might want to consider using an external microphone as well to get crisp and crystal clear audio. Remember audio is very important in a demonstration or sales video.

Make them on Your Computer

You can also make the videos on your computer as well. There are many programs that can make creating your video easy. Camtasia is the most common but it is expensive and might not be required for the casual video creator. There are other less expensive and even a few free programs out there so look around and find the one that is right for you. Each program will have a learning curve associated with it so choose carefully to save yourself time.

The two most common computer generated videos are screen shot videos and power point videos. There are extremely easy to make and should be well within the grasp of nearly every business owner. Both can be effective when used properly. It should be pointed out that neither of these types use real motion video in them so using these as a demonstration video might not be the best idea. But for information purposes, either format should work fine.

Screen shot videos capture an image that is on your monitor and allow you to add audio to it. So you might demonstrate a particular brand of software by creating a video of you actually using the software as you explain that you are doing. Or, if you are explaining anything about how to do something on your computer, these videos work quite well.

PowerPoint videos are slide shows you create on PowerPoint and then add audio to as you go through the slides. So you can have visual items like pictures and text on the screen as you talk. These are great for information type videos as you explain concepts and other how-to information. They are also useful for doing videos on features and benefits and other similar videos.

You can also use a camera and microphone and shoot your own real-time videos using Camtasia or other similar programs. But these require more skill including camera shot set-up. Lighting and other skills that might not be in your wheelhouse. If you go this route I suggest hiring someone to help you. A cheesy or poorly done video will turn off viewers faster than you can hit stop!

Sound for Your Videos

While this might be common sense, the audio in your video will be a major focal point in your video. Audio that is poor, distorted, low volume or otherwise inferior can make even the best shot video difficult to watch and not inspire much confidence.

The built-in microphone on most computers or computer headsets is not a very good choice for your audio. If you are on a strict budget and have no other options you can use it, but an external microphone will make a huge difference in your sound quality.

I purchased an external microphone for about $100 and I have to say it was like night and day when I compared the two videos I made with the new microphone and the headset microphone. The new microphone sound had depth and body to it and was many times clearer than the headset microphone was. It was so much better I actually went back and re-recorded the sound on some older videos to make them much better.

If you are making videos on your computer I suggest a USB microphone which is designed to use one your USB ports and the installation is usually plug and play which is nice as well. If you are using your microphone with a video camera, you would be limited to the ones that are designed for that function. Your other choice is to shoot the video and then re-record the audio on your computer. Unless you are actually on camera talking, you should be able to re-record the audio easily.

Sub-Contract Them

There will always be people willing to make videos for you as long as you provide the content.

Whether or not this makes financial sense to you or not will depend on your particular business and financial situation.

If you do hire someone else to create your videos make certain that you have a license to use all the images and content included in the video and that you own the video and not someone else and that all the images and content is properly licensed to YOU. This will protect you against copyright lawsuits and claims. Ignorance about ownership is NOT a valid defense!

Use Manufacturers Videos

Sometimes other people might have created videos that you would like to use on your site. Examples might be manufacturers who have product demo videos already made. Since there is no reason to duplicate content that is already available, you can import those videos into your website.

Just make sure you are allowed to use their content and be sure to follow the manufacturer's demands as far as showing proper credit for the video if required.

Use Other People's Videos

Also, websites such as YouTube have thousands of videos that you can import and show on your website. All you do is use the program code to import the video and the video will be shown on your website.

While this can be a good thing especially when it comes to relevant content, be sure to watch the videos before choosing them to make sure they are well made, accurate, do not have other people's links inserted into them and most important, do not take viewers away from your page and take them to their page at the end of the video!

If the video is of low quality, or if the content is in poor taste or at all questionable, pass it over and look for another one. Even though the video was made by someone else, you are showing it on your site which means you will be associated with it.

Video Basics

While this is not a book on how to create videos, there are a few important things you should be aware of to protect yourself and get the most out of using video on your website.

First of all, using or creating poor quality video is worse than using no video at all. It doesn't have to be Hollywood quality or even close to that but it can't look like it was created using a 1940's 8mm camera either. It should be clear, easy to watch and at least somewhat impressive.

If you use images in your video make sure that you are licensed to use them. Picking out free images from Google is NOT good enough! Buy your images from low cost sources like depositphoto.com or fotalia.com to avoid any problems. Or, if you are so inclined, take your own pictures and use those.

We mentioned sound before and as we already stated, sound quality is important. Sound should be loud and clear enough for people to be able to hear without straining. If people have to strain to understand or watch a video they will usually just click and go on to something else. So use a good quality microphone.

For computer work USB microphones are easy to use and give good results. For other equipment use the microphone designed to be used for that equipment.

The length of the video is important as well. We are not looking for feature film length videos for our website. Try and get your message across in 2 or 3 minutes. You can go longer if your topic is extremely interesting or if it is content people have subscribed to. But if it is just for use on your sales or home pages, 2 minutes is good.

You probably will be able to have two options when it comes to playing videos. The first is to use a standard player where the viewer hits a play button. The second option is "auto-play" which starts the video automatically after the page loads.

Auto-play is nice when the video is your primary object or focus of your webpage. But if the video is a supporting element of your webpage, auto-play might be distracting to the viewer. If the video is critical to the webpage and starts off the page, then auto-play should work great. It will force the viewer to at least hear the start of the video.

But if the video is a summary or a demonstration of something not previously discussed, then introduce the video further down the page and require the user to press play when they are ready.

Also, video is best used sparingly. Video should complement the content on the page not overwhelm it. Video should be used to create favorable perceptions of the product and the website. It should make the content more interesting and informative and it should benefit the viewer to watch it. If a video does not provide any benefit for the customer to watch it, it shouldn't be on the page in the first place.

Videos allow people to get information more easily and faster than reading a book or a webpage. Any time we give someone a way to accomplish something more easily, customers will probably love it. We all like easy and we all like quick. So if you can produce or find great videos for use on your website, you should be able to increase your business, improve your sales and grow your business.

15. Form Alliances with Other Marketers

Sometimes getting a presence on the web that attracts a lot of followers or visitors can be very difficult. We can do only so much through search engines and advertising, while important to every business, can be expensive and take time to work. But most businesses do not have the luxury of waiting months or even years to get established. They need to generate sales NOW so they can pay expenses NOW!

Sometimes on avenue that might be available to you is to form an "alliance" or a "joint venture" with an establish internet business so you can leverage their name recognition and their customer list to give you a jump start.

There are costs associated with this approach but they can shorten the time necessary to establish yourself by a lot.

In a joint venture what you are essentially doing is paying a portion of your profits to the other partner for being able to access their network of customers. The actual amount is negotiated but usually is around 50% of the cost of the product. While might sound a bit steep, think about one thing for a minute.

Your costs are usually much less than 50% of the cost. So every sale you make you will still make a small profit on. So if you can use someone else's list to generate a few hundred or a few thousand sales, isn't that a great way to get cash flow started NOW rather than waiting for your business to gain traction on its own?

Personally, I would not agree to any commission that is so large that I would lose money on every sale. But if I made a small profit or even broke even on the deal, I would still wind up with a good starting list of customers for my next offer or product release.

Joint ventures are also useful in making early sales so we can gather testimonials and reviews to post on our sales pages. These reviews and testimonials are well known to boost sales, increase customer confidence and give us another way to convince people to purchase.

Another way to achieve sort of the same thing is to join an affiliate network where you allow people to sell your products in exchange for a commission. Programs such as ClickBank and JVZoo are perfect examples. You state which commission you are willing to pay and people search the database to find relevant products to promote on their sites. The program takes a share of the selling price as well for processing sales and commissions.

This can be good because you can have an unlimited number of affiliates advertising your products. But you also lose a bit of control over being able to choose specific people to partner with. It's a trade-off and there is no all that much risk although you never know how someone is going to market your products.

The great part of this arrangement is that you only pay people when they make a sale.

You do not pay them if they place 100,000 ads for your product and don't make a sale. So you only pay for sales or results so on this part there is zero risk. You do not make as much per sale as if you sold it yourself, but you do get a lot more market exposure than you could get by yourself.

If you sell physical products you can even sell on the "giant" websites such as Amazon. I only recommend this for experienced marketers as there is considerable set up and stocking expenses for listing and providing stock to the sellers. But once you get this up and running you can reap the rewards of massive amounts of traffic searching for what you have to sell.

Another way you can get additional exposure is by finding websites where you consider your products a great "fit" and then contacting the owners of those sites and paying them to display your ads. This is extremely targeted traffic as you have personally hand-picked the sites where your ads will be displayed upon.

If you should decide to go this route I would strongly suggest you figure out some way to measure the sales generated from each ad source.

You can use different pages for each site link or different product numbers so you can see where each sale came from. This allows you to know which sites work well and should be continued and which sites produce zero results and should be dropped.

Sometimes you can avoid paying any fees at all and arrange to just swap ads. You run an ad for someone else and they run an ad for you. Just make sure that the ads you are placing on your site are not siphoning sales away from your products. Use links that open in a new window so your site stays on the browser.

The best products for this type of arrangement are complementary products that go well with your products but don't compete with them. This way everyone reaps the benefit of running other people's ads while both people make money in the process.

Whatever arrangement you make with other vendors or other site owners, make sure your interests are protected and that you remain in control of your part of the process.

Make sure that YOU do the order fulfillment so you get a list of everyone who orders. This way you can build your mailing list with these new buyers.

The best deals you make with other people are the deals where everyone makes money. Do not try and cheat other people or swap links and bury there's where no one else will find it. This will create hard feelings and once word gets around, no one will want to deal with you anymore. Go for a win-win situation where everyone is happy and everyone cannot wait until the next deal comes along.

16. Open Multiple Locations!"

Do you know why fast food places sell billions of burgers? They sell that many because they have thousands and thousands of locations all over the country or even the world selling their products! As an on-line business you can do the same thing! This can be a great way to grow your business and increase sales!

If you sell several products, or even if you sell one product that has several different uses or customer types, your business could benefit by opening up a series of targeted websites each one constructed and optimized with just one particular focal point.

Doing this will help you rank higher in search engines and get you more targeted traffic. Since search engines rank sites dedicated to specific products or areas higher than other sites, it makes sense that a site dedicated to one product or one purpose would rank higher and some generic site.

For example, let's say your website sells two primary products. You sell two types on batteries. You sell batteries for commercial tools and another type of homeowner tools. In this example you might want to consider additional sites with one specifically for industrial battery products and another for homeowner level batteries. You would then have one combination site and one specialized site for each application.

You could concentrate the content on each site for specific situations that address each specialty.

You could choose your keywords more accurately and specifically. You can place application specific ads and use application specific videos and other content.

The result would be a site that should rank higher for specific keywords and your group of sites rank higher for a wider range of search terms. You would use links to go from one site to another so your customers would easily be able to find and access your other products.

You could use the same domain and list the other sites as sub-domains or you could use different domain names as well. Whatever you feel will be the most beneficial as long as those domain names are available.

Understand that this is NOT just a way to cheat the search engines. This is a perfectly legal, acceptable and even smart way to construct a website and display your products. The search engines would be happy because each site is totally concentrated on one type of product meaning the person who is directed there has a much higher chance of seeing what they expected or wanted when they were searching.

The website owners get a way to become more targeted while still appealing to a wider range of customers as well. They also benefit in being able to target customers more exactly, choose their monetization options more accurately and that should result in higher income from those sources.

Just like having more locations to sell your products across the country, having more websites to sell your products to targeted customers is a great way to increase your business, grow your sales and reach out to more customers.

17. Deliver Amazing Value

Up to now we have discussed how to bring more people to your website and what to do with them once they get there to convert those visitors into buying customers. But what about what to do once those people become buying customers? Sometimes that is even more important than what you do to get them to buy in the first place!

Once you turn a visitor into a customer, you first thought should be, "Ok, they bought one product from me, now how to I get them to buy from me again?" That is the question most successful businesses ask and it is also the question most failed businesses never even thought about.

What internet business have to create when it comes to fulfilling order sis that all-important "WOW factor!" The "WOW factor" is what impresses or even shocks the customer so much that they cannot wait until they buy from you again. This is precisely why people go back to those "internet giants" for all of their on-line needs!

Any time you can give the customer more than what they thought they were getting, you create a "WOW" factor.

Any time you deliver something to the customer faster than they thought they would receive it you create a "WOW" factor!

Any time customers receive something extra as a surprise or bonus, you create a "WOW" factor!

Any time you do anything more than what the customers expect you create a "WOW" factor!

People who experience a "WOW" factor are far more likely to buy from you again. They are also far more likely to leave positive feedback or leave a testimonial and tell their friends and neighbors about your business.

People who get what they expect are not thrilled with you or your business. After all, you gave them what they expected. You are just like any one of a number of other businesses. Nothing great and nothing bad. Just like all the rest. In other words, nothing to remember you for so the next time a purchase is needed, your business might not be thought of. You possibly lose future sales to others who might have gone a bit above and beyond for their customers.

It is easy to argue against this approach. It costs more to provide more and it takes more time and effort to deliver things better and faster than you normally would. But you cannot place a value on the amount of positive impressions and goodwill marketing you have created.

With the introduction of the internet, our customers have more choices than ever before. It is no longer enough to meet a customer's expectations. A lot of companies do that today. But when you EXCEED what your customer expects that's where the magic comes into play.

The best way to over deliver to your customers is to step back and put yourself in the shoes of the customer. Then take a look at how your business does things.

Is there anything that could be made more customer friendly?

Is there anything that could be made faster?

Are there any processes that could be streamline or improved to make them faster or better in the eyes of the customer?

Is anything you could do for the customer missing from your business?

How does your business compare with other similar businesses? What are you lacking and what do you excel at?

Is there anything that your competition is doing now that you and they were not doing before? Could you ad that now to become more valued in the eyes of the customer?

And here is perhaps the single most important question of all when it comes to your business: "If I were the customer, what would I like to see from this business?"

Successful businesses get to be successful because they operate with the customer as their primary focus. They understand the need to take care of the customer today so that the customer can take care of them tomorrow.

It is a simple concept yet it is completely lost on some businesses today.

Make it a priority to give the customer as much as you possibly can while still maintaining the long term health of the business. Don't just meet the expectations of the customer, blow them away! If they expect A&B, then give them C and possibly D as well. Give them more than they expect so you will make a strong impression and make them remember you the next time they need what you are selling. Make them want to tell their friends and relatives about the treatment they received from you.

A small investment in customer care today can reap huge dividends for you and your business tomorrow. As your business grows, never lose sight of the customer's that enable the growth in the first place. Because without customers, every business fails!

18. Build a List through FREE Products!

When it comes to growing an on-line business, there is a saying that goes something like this: "It's all in your mailing list." What that means is that your mailing list of people who have expressed or shown interest in your products and services is where you make your real money.

Your mailing list is where you go when you need to generate sales or create interest in your products. So instead of starting by scratch every time you release a product or put something on sale, you will have a ready-made tool for promoting your business.

As we have mentioned before, you should make every attempt to get the e-mail address of everyone who visits your site. These are people who have demonstrated at least some interest or need for the products you sell. These are all pre-qualified leads that stand a greater chance of buying from you than regular traffic off the street or even from the search engines.

Think about how great it would be if you create a new product and could immediately send out an e-mail announcing that product and get sales the very same day? Or be able to hold a special or a sale and instantly inform thousands of people about the new offer!

Brick and mortar stores send out catalogs to their customers while on-line store utilize e-mail instead. E-mail is quick, it is cheap and it is effective. The more people on your list, the more prospects you have or readers who will read your next e-mail.

But getting people to join your list can be tricky. No one wants to be overwhelmed with garbage e-mails more commonly referred to as spam. So most people are hesitant to some degree to give up their e-mail address to just anyone.

In order to get someone to give you their e-mail address, you generally have to do two things. First, you have to have compelling content which makes the customer realize that your site has something of value to offer. If they want to get more of that content they will sign up for your newsletter or mailing list. If you content is crap, they won't sign up. It is as simple as that.

But sometimes we need to "sweeten the pot" so to speak and in addition to great content, we need to offer them something as a bonus for giving us their e-mail address. When it comes to giving someone something, everyone loves to get something of value for free. Not at a discount and not for doing much of anything for it. They want stuff for free and we should provide them with something for free in exchange for their e-mail address.

Common "free items" might be reports or e-books, discount coupons for something off their next order, access to special "members only" content and many other things. If you offer something for free, you should get more response from your visitors.

The downside of giving away free stuff for signing up is that you will get people who sign up just to get something for nothing.

They might not have a need for your products or care at all about what you are selling. But by and large there will be some kind of interest just because they wound up on your site in the first place. So when you offer a free gift for signing up, it might dilute the quality of your leads but not all that much.

I have had success offering e-books or report that pertain to my product line or subject matter. Sometimes I give away an overview of something and let the customer know if they want to learn more they can buy the full book at my website. But even the free report is of high quality and does not leave the reader needing to buy the full version to get some benefit from it.

Sometimes websites will offer a complete product for free if the product is part of a collection or series. A perfect example might be a book that is the first book in a series of 7 books. The idea is to give away the first book to get more people exposed to it and hope they like it enough to buy the others in the set. Or maybe a toy that is part of a series so the people buy the rest of the set.

But as we have already stated, be prepared for many people just getting the free product and never buying anything from you.

Some people just get stuff because it's free and then either throw it away eventually, or put it in a drawer where it will soon be forgotten.

The usefulness of the names gathered using free products will depend on the type of product and the offer that is given to the customer. If you offer something of high value, more people will request it and sign up but never buy anything. The number of people actually interested in your products and services are going to depend largely by your content on the site and the traffic you bring to the site.

The use of free offers is just another way to build your list faster. But if you have to rely strictly on the free offer to bribe your customers into signing up, you may wish to revisit either the content on your website or the products that you offer. The whole idea of offering free products is to give your customers a bonus for signing up. Not bribing them to do it.

19. Using E-Mail as a Sales Tool

When you have a mailing list and an effective way of getting people on your list you have the basis for a pretty potent and lucrative way of increasing sales and growing your business. E-mail marketing is something that has sometimes been given a very bad name by scammers and spammers but when used properly can help give your business a good reputation, allow you to showcase your expertise and also give you a built-in audience for the release of new products and services.

Before we get down to how to use e-mail to grow your business and boost your income, let's go over a few things that e-mail should NOT be used for and, if you do these things, will harm your business far more than it will help it.

Getting someone's e-mail address is not an implied consent that it is all right to send them 15 e-mails a day hawking everything from get rich quick schemes to anti-aging miracle drugs. Just because e-mail is cheap does not mean it is OK to abuse those individuals who gave you their address.

E-mail should be used for more than just trying to push your latest product or notify people of your latest sale. If this is all you use it for then you messages will likely be deleted even before they are opened.

Last, but still something you should really be aware of, is that when it comes to e-mail, less is actually more. If you send too many e-mails in a short period of time, you might find yourself on someone's spam or trash folder and then none of your e-mails are actually seen at all! Respect your customer's time and life by not overwhelming them with e-mails!

OK, now that we have that out of the way, e-mail is a great way to deliver messages and information as well as sale notifications and other sales related materials. It is targeted because people have signed up for your list from your site and they must have at least some interest because they got to your site in the first place.

So I think we can agree that when used properly, e-mail can be a great tools to help grow your business and sales. With that in mind, here are a few things to think about when using e-mail and your customer mailing list:

Always have a good reason to send the e-mail. If you don't have anything worthwhile to say, then don't send out the e-mail. It sounds simple but a lot of businesses fail to adhere to this. We all get e-mails with just links or cryptic messages that supposedly get you to click that link. Very few people click those links and a lot of people ban the senders so if you don't have something of value to say, don't send out any e-mails.

Second, always have something the benefits the customer in the e-mail. That might be useful information or tips and advice or anything that the reader will find useful and valuable.

This is important because as long as your e-mails have useful content, your customers will continue to open them and read them. If the content is excellent all of the time people might actually look forward to getting e-mails from you. If you can achieve that with your e-mails you will get a LOT of sales and a LOT of growth!

Third, keep your e-mails limited to the type of subject or products that your customers sought when they signed up in the first place. If you sell computer products don't try to promote acne cream to your readers. That will just annoy them. Stick to what you know they are interested in. The only exception might be if you find a product or service that is an exceptional value or product that would make a major positive improvement in people's lives.

For example, if I sell clothing and I find a wonderful credit security service for a really good price and I know many people would benefit from it, I might make my customers aware of that service if there has been recent problems with on-line security. That product is sort of related because it involved on-line transactions and it can help people.

But even in this case, I would not do this very often. Once or twice a year tops. You want to keep your e-mails focused on what you know the customers are interested in.

Fourth, give something to your subscribers once in a while. Give them a special discount or even a free product on occasion so they continue to see value in the e-mails and will always open them. Remember, even the best crafted e-mail will not accomplish a thing if it is never opened! Providing value and unannounced bonuses helps get e-mails opened and read!

Fifth, time is money for most people and no one likes to read e-mails that read like novels. Get to the point and deliver your message quickly using as few words as possible while still making it readable and delivered in the tone you want. In other words, if you can send a good e-mail that delivers your message in 150 words, don't use 1,500 words to say the same thing. Most long winded e-mails are just deleted anyway.

Sixth, make you e-mails easy to read and easy to take action with.

If you want someone to click on a certain link, make sure the address appears as a link that can be clicked on and not just regular text that has to be copied. The easier it is for someone to do something the more likely those people will actually do it!

Seventh, limit your e-mails to one or two per week if that many. If people see too many e-mails from you they might wonder why you need to send so many e-mails. Instead, create some anticipation and send out one a week or a couple a month instead. Always make sure you have good content and good reason for sending the e-mail. If that is lacking, skip the e-mail.

Eighth, don't make every e-mail about buying something. Keep some e-mails information based to show the customer that you want to help them and provide them information and not just sell them things. Your customer's will appreciate this and think more highly of you and your business.

Ninth, always provide a way for people to opt-out of your list whenever they want. Some e-mail services require this but even if they don't it is something customers appreciate having even though most will never use it.

Having the opt-out link in every e-mail at the bottom just makes your business look and feel more legitimate and trustworthy.

Tenth, if you want to get more names in your list, you have to make it easy. Double opt-in, which requires a second e-mail confirming they signed up, will make the list harder to join and reduce your overall number of sign-ups. The same holds true for the information required to sign-up. At the minimum you need the e-mail address but some ask for the first and last name as well. The first name is good for automatic personalization but the last name is not needed for much of anything. The less information the customer has to give the more likely they will be to sign up.

E-mail is also a good tool to use for after sale follow-up. These e-mails can be sent out to customers a day or so after the purchase has been made to make sure everything has gone along fine with their purchase. This is one good reason to ask people for their e-mail address when they purchase. Depending on your product or industry, you might send weekly follow-up e-mails with information on how to best use their products or training and tips to make things work better or easier.

If you don't use e-mail as a marketing tool you are missing out on a great way to stimulate sales, increase profits and facilitate the growth of your business. Done and used properly, e-mail will make growing your business easier and faster.

Bot only when used properly.

20. Create a Blog

If you have information or commentary to share regarding your business or just the industry or market that you are in, perhaps you should consider starting a blog. Blogs are websites that allow you to post comments, accept comments from others and share information and news about any topic you desire.

It used to be that blogs looked like, well, blogs. The structure was pretty much the same although the pictures and payouts could be changed. But today there are editors and plug-ins that allow anyone to create a blog that looks just like a "regular" website. More of that in a bit.

Blogs are interesting for business use because they allow others to create your content and that content might be very much in demand in your particular market. Chances are the thoughts and comments posted by some of your readers will be close to, or pretty much the same as, other people who are reading your blog. So the answers will be valuable to more than just the person asking the question or giving the opinion.

While this allows other people to add to your content, you should be aware that posts by others will not always be in your best interests. Some might recommend other products or websites and some might even trash your product or website. In fact, there are some marketers who teach courses on how to market your products on other people's blogs!

For this reason, I suggest you set up your blog so that you personally have to approve all posts to your blog before they appear on your live blog. This allows you to delete spam comments or comments that are negative in nature while allowing you to pass on good comments and posts to your readers. While this is a form of censorship it is your blog and you are allowed to have some control over the content that appears on it.

The advantage of a blog is that it is easy to set up and run and requires only the most basic of technical skills to operate. Installation is straight from your webhosts control panel and the installation is usually automated for you. All you have to do is make a few mouse clicks and enter a user name and password to access the blog.

WordPress is by far the most popular blog format and all the plug-ins and accessories for blogs are made to be compatible with WordPress. Adding a feature to your blog is as easy as installing a plug-in for that feature and that is done with a few mouse clicks as well.

Blogs also have a certain amount of search engine optimization built in and search engines usually like blogs that are active and provide valued content. But in order to get a good search engine ranking you need to keep your blog active which means regularly posting to your blog to keep the content fresh.

One easy way to keep content fresh is to use the same content you use in your informational e-mails. If you are writing an informational e-mail just copy the text and paste it into a blog post.

This gets the same information sent to your e-mail list to other people as well. This results in a wider audience for your message. Be careful not to send out "members only" posts to your blog, however!

As we already mentioned, there are WordPress Editors available that let you throw away the "old" WordPress formats and create pages that look any way you would like them to look. You do not have to have any programming skills to use these editors so your format is limited only to your imagination!

Blogs are just another way for you to get your information to a larger and wider audience. Blogs might get ranked higher than you regular website and this might help you get more search engine traffic. For this reason ALWAYS include a link to your primary website on every page of your blog so it is easy for viewers to go to your website for more information.

You will find the overall flexibility of a blog to be very large. Though it might seem a bit daunting in the beginning, let me assure you that it is a very straightforward and easy process once you get a little used to it.

There are many online tutorials on WordPress and there are plug-ins for almost any function you could think of.

You can add payment systems, membership sites, member's only areas, list building tools and huge number of other plug-ins to help you build your business and grow your customer list. You could operate your blog for years and still not be totally aware of everything it could do for you!

When it comes to blogs, there are a few things you should be aware of.

First, unlike your website which is designed on your computer and uploaded to the internet, blogs are hosted and edited on-line. This has advantages and disadvantages.

The advantages are that the whole site is hosted on the internet which means if your computer crashes of your home catches fire, your site information is hosted remotely and remains intact and you can recover it remotely. When you lose your website files you must either attempt to download them back from the internet (not all that straightforward) or start from scratch.

The disadvantage is that unless you back up your entire blog after you make changes, you will not have a back-up file should your webhosts server go down or get hacked. So if you are putting a lot of time and effort into creating the perfect blog, make sure you back it up regularly to your hard drive in case something bad happens.

Blogs are also more vulnerable to hackers in some cases because common themes, once hacked, can be easily hacked on other sites. WordPress is very good at updating their system to address these issues so when you are notified that a new version of WordPress is available, update your installation immediately. You can update without losing your design or any files. It takes just seconds.

Because of the same platform, I urge you to use very secure usernames and passwords. Don't use "admin" and "password" as your log-in information like a lot of people do. Keep passwords easy to remember but complex enough to make it difficult for someone to guess or figure out. That means no passwords that include birthdays, children's name, anniversaries, person name, spouse's name or anything like that. Mix up letters, numbers and add at least one symbol if not more.

If you allow posts and comments from others be aware that once you publish that information on your blog you become at least partially liable for that content. So delete any posts or comments that are false or misleading, racist or obscene or even questionable in content. Posts that defame or are derogatory towards any individual or group should be banned as well. If in doubt, leave it out!

As far as updating your blog is concerned, you can update it as often as you want because people will only see those comments and posts when they visit your blog. It is not like bombarding their inbox every day. But keep your posts short and sweet and only post when you have something of value to say. If that is once a day, that's fine. If it's once a week or once a month, that's OK too. But remember that you want people to come back so you should add new content and posts from time to time to give people that reason to come back.

Do not think of your blog as a second rate version of your website or business. Give it the time and attention it deserves. Remember some people will come to your blog first and then go to your website if they are interested.

Others will come to your website first and go to your blog if they are interested as well. So make sure both your blog and your website are functional, well thought out and designed and attractive.

One last thing about blogs.

Blogs are cheap as they can be run on your primary domain or even for free on some of the blog hosting services. So that means you can have more than one blog if you cater to more than one type of customer. Create a blog for every type of customer or any type of interest that is common for your customers. This will give them a special place to go to get the information they need from your business.

Free or Self-Hosted?

Free blog hosting services will allow you to create your own blog for free and have it hosted by them. They are usually free easy to set up and most have a point and click set up process. But even though they are free does not mean it is the best option for you.

Free blogs will limit your flexibility when it comes to appearance and design.

You usually cannot add plug-ins to free blogs unless those are plug-ins they feature as options. For example if you wish to add a payment processor, you could do that easily on a self-hosted blog but not on a free blog.

With FREE blogs you name choices might be limited as well. If the desired name is already taken, you cannot use it again. You would have to change the name on your blog and that might create confusion among your customers. Also, your name might be too long or too short for a FREE blog and that can cause the same issues.

FREE blogs also might place ads or other information on your blog and this is how they make money and can furnish FREE blogs to people like you and I. This can lessen the professional appearance of your blog. When customers see "Hosted by XYZ Free Blog Service" on your webpage it sends the message that you are too cheap to publish your own blog. This can negatively impact how people feel about your blog.

If you host your own website, which the vast majority of businesses do, it is far better and a lot more professional for you to host your own blogs as well.

You can set them up as sub-domains in a different folder. (Do NOT set up your blog in the primary, or root, of your domain or it will REPLACE your website! Use a structure like the following:

Primary website: Yourdomain.com

First Blog: Yourdomain.com/blog1

Second Blog: Yourdoamin.com/blog2

This will allow you to run a separate website and unlimited blogs all on one domain. So there will be no additional cost to run your blogs, you will be able to name it whatever you wish, there will be no other ads or words on your blog except for the ones you place on it and you will have the flexibility and creativity to do whatever you want with any of your blogs!

21. Include Reviews or Testimonials on Your Site

Part of the problem we have as internet businesses is that we don't really have a way to "talk up" our products and service to our customers. Instead we have to depend on carefully worded descriptions and some pictures or images. But sometimes this isn't enough.

But if we have product reviews with comments and testimonials from actual customers or users, those could be a determining factor in convincing people to purchase the products from you.

Reviews are descriptions of how well or poorly the product works and how accurately the product was described on the website. In other words, it tells people if the product is any good, what is good or bad about it, and how satisfied the customer was overall. Reviews can be positive, negative or neutral. Most websites use a star based system with one star being poor and 5 stars being great. This lets people express a wide range of opinions and other information. For example, a review might be something like this:

"The XQ-47 sound system delivers great sound and is easy to set up and use. It has enough power to fill even larger rooms and the sound is very clear and life-like. The remote buttons are a little small but you get used to that in a day or so. I give it 4 stars only because of the remote."

Testimonials, on the other hand, tend to be more positive and about the product and the business. These generally come from (or are supposed to come from) actual customers. A testimonial may also have nothing what so ever to do with the product and be just about the business. For example a testimonial might be something like:

"I bought the XQ-47 sound system from Dave's Electronics and they were excellent. Delivery was fast, people were helpful and they even called me the next week to make sure everything was great! I would buy from them anytime!"

Your website should have a few product reviews whenever possible for every product you sell. They should be on the same page as the product so they can be easily seen. Testimonials, on the other hand, are usually on the home page so everyone can see them. But if a testimonial mentions a specific product along with your business you might want to include a few testimonials on the product pages as well.

Reviews and testimonials help provide depth and realism to the products as well as more accurately describe how great your business is. When used correctly, they can inspire confidence, remove apprehension and doubt and increase the likelihood of the customer purchasing the product from your business and not somewhere local.

It should be mentioned at this point that all testimonials and product reviews should be from actual customers or users and reflect their real and truthful comments.

You should never create your own fake testimonials to make your products or business appear better than it really is.

This is a common practice with many sites and the result is loss of credibility and higher customer dissatisfaction. If someone sees a glowing testimonials or review and they get a piece of garbage after they order, they are not going to be happy with you. Once word gets around your credibility will be damaged and sometimes businesses never recover from that kind of damage.

Another temptation is to only post positive reviews and testimonials. As far as reviews are concerned, there will always be at least a few negative reviews as some people find fault with almost everything and will post a negative review if the product isn't something that answered their every whim and made all their dreams come true. So people expect to see some negative reviews. If they see 1,500 5 star or 4 start reviews and no negatives, they will get suspicious.

For testimonials, it is all right to just use the positive ones. People expect this on a website or in a print ad. But if you get some negative comments, do not just throw them away.

Think about those comments and see what you could do to change things to eliminate or reduce the chances of this happening again. Of course, if the comment is really off the wall and lacks common sense, you can throw those away!

Testimonials can also be listed on their own page if you have enough of them. People usually place 2 or 3 on their home page to inspire confidence but if you have a lot of really nice comments from customers you can always list them on their own page and provide a link on your home page for customers to click on. Then they can read as few or as many as they feel like without getting annoyed that all of these testimonials are getting in the way of them reading what they need to read. Testimonials should always be used as a positive force and never as a distraction or as an inconvenience to the customer.

The same goes for reviews. Add a few reviews from every level and just give a total of all the reviews. All we need is a good representation of what the product is and what the customers can expect.

22. Outsource It!

There are a LOT of different skills needed to operate a successful on-line business. There is product creation or selection, marketing, web design, graphics creation, site coding and who knows what else you particular business requires to operate successfully. It is a rare person who can excel at everything but many still insist on trying!

In the beginnings when money was tight and time was plentiful, most of us struggled through doing whatever was required to get through the next step.

We learned how create a basic website to get some presence on the web. We developed crude graphics on Photoshop or some other graphics program.

We might have even "borrowed" a graphic or two from the internet. The result might not have been pretty but it got us started.

But now we are looking to expand our business, reach more people, improve our image and sell more products. Which means we have to look better, operate smoother and deliver a better experience for our customers. In many cases this is going to require better quality skills and more time to accomplish all of this.

So we have a choice to make. We can continue to do everything ourselves and for some of us, this might work. But for most of us, the sheer amount of time required to do all the things we need to do and do them the right way would be too much to fit into our schedules.

Even if we could still manage to spend all that time doing the things that need to get done, it would still take away our time from developing new products, managing the business or just keeping an eye on how things are going and other day to day things that are part of running a well-organized business.

As your business grows, you need to re-evaluate whether it still makes sense for you to continue doing certain things. In some cases, it might be cheaper to get the work done by other people who are more skilled and can do the same things in less time and come out with much better results!

For example, if you can pay something $25 to create a beautiful graphic or logo, would that be worth it to you? It might take you 5 hours to get something that looks half as good! Is your time worth more than $5 an hour? Could you utilize that time doing things that would generate MORE income than that $25?

Let's also talk about another aspect of time. If you have 20 things to do and they need to be done quickly, does it make sense for you to do all 20 things yourself even if you are capable of doing them yourself? Or, would it make sense to have 5 people each handle 4 of those things and get them done all in one or two days?

So much about business is time sensitive. Sometimes being the first one to market a product can result in huge sales. But if you take longer to do things yourself you might miss out on some critical opportunities.

The bottom line is that you should be running your business. Your business should not be running you! Spend your time doing the things related to your business that you like to do and are very good at. Let the other stuff get done by other people so your can free up more of your time for growing your business and making new plans.

Yes, it will cost you some money and if you don't have that money you might have to re-think your plans. But if you have the money, and you want to expand, consider outsourcing some of the tasks involved to others so you can do what is best for your business.

Still be involved, still approve and monitor the work that other people do for you but let go of some of the little things and concentrate on what you do best.

There are many sites where you can find people to partner with you or do work for a fee. If you have enough work you might even take on an employee or maybe even a partner. Just make sure the work they produce is quality work that represents your business well. A poorly done graphic or a website design that is ugly or non-functional; is not worth it no matter how cheap the price was.

Search for quality people, ask to see examples of your work and give them a couple of small jobs at first to see how they do. If they do a great job then trust them with more of your work.

There is one thing to always be aware of when subcontracting work to others. The more details or information you give other people about your business and your products, the more likely they will be to steak from you. Your new product could be stolen right before release and that new web design might include a few photos that are not licensed.

No matter who did the work it is YOUR name on the business and YOUR business that will suffer the fall-out if things are not done correctly. You MUST remain aware and in-charge and have final authority on what is done, when it is done and how it is done.

It is YOUR business and don't let someone else damage it or steal it away from you!

23. Brick & Mortar Stores

Chances are if your products sell well online there will be a need for them in regular storefronts as well. In fact, with some people always preferring to purchase locally where they can see and touch the products before buying them, you might be able to tap into a whole other group of customers if you open a real storefront.

Another advantage is that when people buy from a physical location, most of the time they walk out with their purchase tucked under their arm or in a bag. They don't have to wait for shipping or delivery. Sometimes this is a huge incentive for people to purchase locally.

Brick and Mortar stores require a LOT more money to set up and maintain. You will have rent and utilities, stock charges, employees to pay and a host of other expenses your on-line store doesn't have. But depending on the type of products you see and the area in which you would sell them, expanding into a storefront just might make a lot of sense for you and your business.

If you decide to go in this direction, be as sure as you can that this is a good idea and that the market has a need for what you are selling. You can put a website up for $50 and if it fails you are out $50. Most of us can deal with that. But it is an entirely different story when you have $250,000 invested and your business fails! So be careful, do your research, look to see how similar businesses are doing in this market before you make any commitments.

24. Franchising

If your business has a solid and well known reputation, and you are known to have a great business model that works well, perhaps you can expand by offering other people the ability to buy into your business and use your name.

Franchising can allow you to use other people's money to fund your expansion in return for a share of the profits that the business generates. While it is not as profitable as owning your own stores and keeping all the profits, using other people's money takes a lot of the risk away from you and allows you to grow faster than if you had to pay for everything yourself.

Franchisees get the ability to market and sell your products and services in exchange for paying you, the parent company, a fee based on the amount of sales. If you manufacture your own products this can great increase your sales of products as well.

Franchising works best when you sell products and services that have a broad appeal across a wide geographical area. The great part about franchising is that your brand recognition gets a lot better and the franchise owners get almost instant credibility by using an existing name.

If you think franchising is a possibility for your business in the future I urge you to get some professional assistance so you can find out more about the process. You should also hire a good lawyer with experience in franchising to create your contracts and protect you and your business from possible actions of the franchisees.

25. Avoid Over Extension

Everyone says that having too many sales or too much business is a great problem to have. After all, making too much money is never a bad thing, right? Well, not all the time. In fact, growing too fast, too quickly can cause a LOT of problems for a business both long and short-term.

When a business is equipped to handle a certain amount of orders or manufacturing and all of a sudden those levels are doubled or tripled, several things can happen.

Quality control goes way down as production is hurried or rushed. The result are more quality related problems and possible customer dissatisfaction because of these defects. This can lead to more returns, refund and exchanges and an overall poor image of you and your business.

Processing time increases because there are not enough people to handle the extra volume. You might run out of boxes or supplies and this will result in further delays. The result is that people who would normally get their orders within a week might now wait 4-6 weeks and think that this is normal for your business. The result is a poor image for your business.

If you purchase products from vendors, they might not be able to keep up with the demand and this will result in even larger delays for the customer. Your business might not be able to pay upfront for products needed to fulfill orders as well.

Growth is wonderful but only when the business can assume control over such growth. While there will be times when a business might struggle to keep up with an unexpected demand for a certain product, these situations are unavoidable.

When it comes to handling growth that is entirely something else.

In order to remain successful and grow your business, it is always better to have a well thought out plan instead of just diving in head first and hoping for the best. Growth is one of those areas where more is sometimes not better. So let's give some thought about how the best way to go about growing our business should be.

Before we make any decisions based on how we operate our business, we need to identify all the "players" involved and what their roles would be in our growth. This way we can address everyone's roles and responsibilities now rather than later.

For example, if we deal with a vendor and we think our growth would triple our need for products, we should consult the vendor to find out if they are capable of handling that much material, how it will effect fulfillment or delivery time, and what problems, if any, might be encountered.

Within our company, we have our own involvement which must be analyzed and evaluated as well. We should ask ourselves if our current manpower and structure could handle a 300% increase in orders.

If it can, that's great! But if it can't then we have to determine what needs to be done to make sure it can handle such a dramatic increase. Maybe we need to hire more people, perhaps we need to order more equipment, increase our warehouse space or any of the other many things that might be impacted by our expansion.

It is better to plan these things out so we can decide if we are ready or if we need to scale back our plans so that we can take care of our new and old customers at the level as we did before. It is better to slow growth and maintain service levels than try and do too much and damage customer relationships.

Try to keep in mind that not only sales and fulfillment are effected by growth. As more orders come in there will be more requests for support or refunds or inquiries regarding accounts. All of those departments need to be evaluated as well.

If our business takes orders over the phone then do we have enough people manning the phones to insure a quick response time so people do not hang up and purchase something or somewhere else? If we outsource this part of the task doe to vendor handling our phone calls have additional people on hand to take our calls?

Making a lot of money is great and it can be exciting and fun. But if we try to do too much too soon, we might be trading short-term success for long-term damage to our reputation. That is not a good trade to make.

Naturally sometimes the situation is a no brainer. If you sell digital products such as e-books or reports and these are delivered automatically, then you really don't have to worry about order fulfillment because all of that is handled within your software.

But even then you might have to make sure your site can handle all the extra traffic and that you will not be exceeding any bandwidth restrictions on your web account. That might result in the shutting down of your account once bandwidth is exceeded or at least being charged extra fees for the added bandwidth.

We are not trying to discourage people on trying to grow their business. What we are trying to do is make sure you think about the entire process, and the expected results carefully. In some cases it might be good to proceed as planned while in other cases it might be better to scale back things a bit and grow in a more controlled and slower manner.

There is no cookie cutter approach and everyone's situation will be different. The only thing we can do is look at as much of the situation as we can and try to make educated and informed decisions. Will there be surprises along the way? Of course there will. But the more we plan, the more we investigate and the more we anticipate, the more we limit those surprises and we become more informed and more prepared every day.

26. Do Something You Love!

Perhaps this should have been number one but I thought I should make this the last way for you to grow your business. Not because it might be the most lucrative choice for you but because building something that revolves around what you love in life will give you the most fulfillment and the best chance for success.

Operating and building any kind of business takes work. Sometimes it takes a lot of work and more often than not, money will cease to be the primary driver or motivator for the business owner.

While money is nice, its effect as a motivator is temporary at best. Most people need something more.

When you build a business around something that you love, or something that has meaning, much of the work is not really work at all. It becomes a passion. It becomes something you enjoy doing not something you have to do. The result is that when people do something they love, or something they find fulfilling, they remain committed to it for longer period of time.

All businesses have their ups and downs. In the beginning the downs may exceed the ups and that is when commitment comes into play. Sometimes success is just one action or one decision away and only those who remain committed actually get to the point of making those decisions in their lives. Others quit before they reach that point.

Another reason is that running an online business and sharing your knowledge and wisdom can only occur when you have acquired that knowledge and wisdom in the first place. Much of that knowledge will most probably come from actually doing what you are writing about and sharing your experiences and tips on the subject.

If you love video gaming, for example, and you sell video games, you can inform your customers on how to best win a game or which game systems are the best and why because you actually play them on a daily basis. While others can just write from what it says on the sell sheet, you can write because you have done it!

The same can be said for any topic or any product. If you love doing something or using something, you are naturally going to have more knowledge. If you have more knowledge you will become more valuable because you will have more to share.

People like to share their passions and what drives them with others. Your customers will see your passion and commitment from your website. It will come across in your posts or articles and in your recommendations and product selections. Your customers will get the value from dealing with you because you love what you are doing and will do whatever you need to make your business better.

You don't do it because you have to. You do it because you want to.

So even though there will be times when your business gets you down, you will never lose commitment or your passion. Because what you do for work is not really work at all.

And that, my friends, is when you know you are a success.

In Conclusion

We have covered a lot of material in this report and we hope it has been informative and even a little eye opening. Not that we want to scare you, though. We just want to make you aware so that you can be prepared. Id we have accomplished just that, then this report has been worthwhile.

There are a lot of factors that go into whether or not any business is successful. But if you had to boil it all down to a short and simple statement, I guess it would be this:

"Businesses who provide what their customers are looking for and do it in an informative and easy manner will usually become the most successful"

That means listening to your customers so that you KNOW what they want and don't have to guess. It means accepting their praise because you know what you are doing right and taking their criticism because that tells you what you are doing wrong or what you need to do better.

Unless you are in the wonderful position of being the only business selling a particular product or service, you are not going to become successful relying only on the products you sell. Your customers can get them elsewhere and never know the difference.

But if you can deliver those same exact products better, faster, friendlier and with a higher level of trust and confidence then you won't have to plan for growth because grow will come to you.

In fact, that is the very best way to grow. By listening to what your customers say about you and your business and always trying to make things easier and better for the customer. This is when customers tell others and your reputation starts to spread among friends and neighbors and you get noticed in forums and blogs.

You never know when the next huge customer is going to hear about you from someone who made a tiny purchase but was impressed by your service and the entire experience.

Even the tiniest sale can turn into the largest customer or the best marketing tool your business has ever seen. Remember that every business on the internet started out where you are today. They grew into giants because customers liked what they did and how they did it. It's not always about price and most of the time price is not even number two on the list. What is most important is the overall customer experience that you provide.

When your customers want to come back, you have achieved success. When they HAVE to come back, that means you now have a second change to impress them. Do what you have to in order to impress your customers because that is where the very best source of future growth will come.

Other Publications Available From 26Ways.com:

26 Ways to Save Money on Your Utility Bills

26 Ways to Get More Fun From RC Aircraft

For more information and the latest Titles please go to our Website at:

http://www.26ways.com

www.ingramcontent.com/pod-product-compliance
Lightning Source LLC
Chambersburg PA
CBHW071758200526
45167CB00017B/407